The Syro-Malabar Rite

Analecta Gorgiana

138

Series Editor
George Kiraz

Analecta Gorgiana is a collection of long essays and short monographs which are consistently cited by modern scholars but previously difficult to find because of their original appearance in obscure publications. Carefully selected by a team of scholars based on their relevance to modern scholarship, these essays can now be fully utilized by scholars and proudly owned by libraries.

The Syro-Malabar Rite

Archdale King

gorgias press

2009

Gorgias Press LLC, 180 Centennial Ave., Piscataway, NJ, 08854, USA

www.gorgiaspress.com

Copyright © 2009 by Gorgias Press LLC

Originally published in 1948

2009   ≺

ISBN 978-1-60724-102-7

This is an extract from Archdale King's *The Rites of Eastern Christendom*, Vol. 2, Chapter IX.

Printed in the United States of America

SYRO-MALABAR RITE

A lonely outpost of primitive Christianity is found on the western coast of south India, where there are native Catholics who claim spiritual descent from St. Thomas the Apostle.

The district extends from Trivandrum to Calicut, although their traditional home was from Chattanoor, south of Quilon, to Kunankalam, north of Cochin territory.

Malabar or *Male* ("mountain"), as the country was anciently called, has Malayalam for the vernacular language, which is a Dravidic (not Aryan) dialect nearly akin to Tamil.

History

All local tradition has identified St. Thomas, sometimes accompanied by St. Bartholomew, as the apostle of the country, and his preaching in India has been attested by St. Ephrem, St. Ambrose, St. Paulinus of Nola, St. Jerome, and many others.

The chief source for the Indian apostolate of St. Thomas is the *Acta Thomae,* a Syrian document of Gnostic origin, probably dating from the first quarter of the 3rd century, and prompted by the translation of the saint's body to Edessa. It has been quoted as authentic by Eusebius, [1] Epiphanius [2]

[1] *Hist. Eccles.,* III, 25.
[2] *Haer.,* XLVII, 1.

and Gregory of Tours,[3] but it betrays a Manichean bias, speaking as if Christianity and virginity were necessarily identical terms. Eusebius says on hearsay that Pantaenus,[4] founder of the Alexandrine catechetical school, preached in India, where St. Bartholomew had visited, and that he discovered Christians who were in possession of a Hebrew[5] version of the Gospel of St. Matthew. St. Jerome,[6] also, writes of Pantaenus as instructing "the Brahmins and philosophers of that people."

The apostolate of St. Thomas in India has had many defenders, in addition to the natives themselves, Thus, in 1745, a supporter was found in Raulin; while Paulinus a S. Bartolomeo in an unpaged manuscript (1785), preserved in the Vatican library, has written: *"Hanc opinionem etiam hic Christiani Malabaresi firma, stabili, ac plena traditione sustinent."* All the Christians in the country are spoken of as St. Thomas Christians or *Mar Thoma Nazranikal* (*Nazranis*), although this title has been specially claimed by a schismatic and heretical sect. One writer, in referring to the name, somewhat naively said that such a designation denotes the presence of Christianity in the country prior to the time when the Nazarenes were first called Christians at Antioch!

Nazrani Mapila[7] is another title which is given to the Christians of the country, taking its name from the two Malayalam words, *maha* ("great") and *pilla* ("son").

Pope Leo XIII, in the apostolic letter *Humanae Salutis Auctor* (September 1, 1886), says of St. Thomas: *"Atque*

[3] *Miracul. Liber,* I, 32.
[4] † ab. 200.
[5] i. e. Syriac.
[6] *Epist.* LXX *ad Magn. Orat.*
[7] The name, which designates "royal princes," was first given to Thomas of Cana, and later applied to all Christians.

sequentibus saeculis post ipsam errorum luctuosam propagationem nequaquam est deleta memoria ejus, itemque fides quam ille disseminaret .... non extincta funditus esse visa est." In 1923 (December 21), Pope Pius XI issued the bull *Romani Pontifices,* authorising the appointment of native diocesan bishops for the Catholics of the Malabarese rite. St. Thomas, in this document, is called the "Apostle of India," but neither the character nor the extent of his apostolate is defined.

The *Acta Thomae* say that St. Thomas [8] landed at Sandrok Mahosa [9] or Cranganore, a town dedicated to the god Siva. [10] Tradition asserts that the saint founded seven churches in Malabar-Quilon, Niranam, Chayal (Nilakal), Kokamangalam, Kottakavu (north Parur), Cranganore (Kodungalloor), Palur. He is said to have suffered martyrdom [11] on the Big Mount, eight miles from Mylapore. [12] "Holy Mylapore" was destroyed during the persecution of the

---

[8] The Jacobite writer, Bar Hebraeus, has left us a picturesque story relating to the Indian apostolate of St. Thomas. Thus, the apostle had been enjoined by the Holy Spirit to preach the gospel in India, but, on account of the barbarian people, he was reluctant to do so. While hesitating, Habban, a merchant sent by the king of the Indies, appeared in the country, and St. Thomas was led by Christ to visit him. The merchant, at the instigation of our Lord, "bought" St. Thomas and took him back to India, where he was commissioned by the king to build a palace. The gold, however, that he was given for the purpose he gave to the poor and needy, and the saint was imprisoned. A vision of the "Jewish slave" building a magnificent palace, which came to the sick brother of the king, brought about his immediate release and return to favour. The king and his brother both embraced the Christian religion, while the gospel was preached freely throughout the kingdom. *Ap. Malabar. Dict. d'Archéol. Chrét. et de Lit.,* t. X, col. 1260.

[9] Muziris of the Greeks; Musiri of the Tamil classics; Muyirikkodu of the Cochin copper-plate Jewish charter of 1095.

[10] Sandrok through the Sanskrit refers to Siva.

[11] The same tradition says that St. Thomas was killed with a spear.

[12] Tamil, "Town of peacocks;" Tirumailapur.

Christians that followed the revival of Brahminism in the 7th century. It was rebuilt, but by 1500 the town was once again little more than a heap of ruins. The Portuguese, however, in 1522 discovered the alleged tomb of the apostle, with certain small relics now preserved in the cathedral o. Saint-Thomas-of-Mylapore. The Roman martyrology, combining several legends, relates that St. Thomas, after preaching the gospel to the Parthians, Medes, Persians and Hyrcanians, passed into India, and was there martyred at "Calamina." There has been no satisfactory identification of this place, but, when Cosmas visited India in the 6th century, he said: "There is a Christian Church in Male where the pepper grows. In another place called Caliana a bishop appointed in Persia resides." The relics of the apostle seem to have been translated [13] from somewhere to Edessa early in the 3rd century, and in 232 a great festival was held there to celebrate their arrival. An early Syrian calendar has the entry: "3 July, [14] St. Thomas who was pierced with a lance in India. His body is at Urhai (Edessa), having been brought there by the merchant Khabin. A great festival." These relics were later moved to the island of Chios and from thence to the church of Ortona [15] in the Abruzzi, where they are still venerated. Mylapore, as we have seen, claims some relics of the saint, and his tomb there was an object of pilgrimage, especially on the first Sunday after Easter, until the *Padroado* troubles occasioned

[13] Bar Hebraeus (*Chronicon*, I, 66) says that the translation took place under Bishop Eulogius (378-388).

[14] Under the same date, the Roman martyrology says: "At Edessa in Mesopotamia, the translation from India of St. Thomas the Apostle, whose relics were afterwards translated to Ortona."

[15] On December 21, 1943, the feast of the apostle, the cathedral church was destroyed by the Germans to provide a road-block against the advancing English. The relics were unharmed.

by the bull [16] of Pope Gregory XVI, when the dioceses under the royal patronage of Portugal in the British territories of India were suppressed, caused the popularity of the shrine to wane.

The supporters of the theory that St. Thomas preached only in *north* India maintain that the body of the apostle was removed to Parthian Persia when the countries of the Indus ceased to be under Parthian rule, and to Roman Edessa when Persia became Zoroastrian. St. Gregory of Tours, [17] writing before 690, speaks of a pilgrim named Theodore, who related that where the body of Thomas the Apostle had first rested there now stood a monastery and a church of striking dimensions and elaborately adorned, adding that "after a long interval of time these remains had been removed thence to the city of Edessa." St. Ephrem in the forty-second *Carmina Nisibiana,* supports both the Indian apostolate of St. Thomas and the translation of his relics. A theory has been put forward of late years, reinforced by the old legend of the conversion by St. Thomas of the Parthian king Gundaphares, to the effect that the apostle who came from Socotra to Malabar was Bar Tolmai (St. Bartholomew), not Mar Thomas, and that the latter confined his work to north India, only coming south spiritually and in the wake of the Pahlavi power. Thus, Pantaenus seems to know nothing about the presence of St. Thomas in Malabar; while Philostorius (ab. 450) says that "the innermost Indians [18] had been converted by Bartholomew, which Indians had formerly been Sabaens or Himyarites." By 883, the Church of Malabar had become that of "the Apostles

---

[16] *Multa praeclare,* 1838.
[17] *Glor. Mart.*
[18] It has been suggested, however, that the "Indians" were inhabitants of Arabia.

Bartholomew and Thomas," later dropping the "Bartholomew."

What one may call the north Indian thesis is supported
by the fact that the Syrian traffic in Chinese silk reached its
climax in the 1st century of our era, and that Peshawar,
the centre of Gundaphares' territory, was an important
market for the two countries.

Emigration southward is said to have taken place with
Peshawar as a starting point, and the parent script of the
south Indian alphabet appears to be Sabaean, [19] derived from
the Phoenician.

If Christian converts of St. Thomas had shared in this
trek, then very probably they were joined later by sufferers
from the Sassanid persecutions in Persia (226-462), and the
two immigrations from the north were thus united with those
who had come direct from Syria to Malabar. Teak beams
found in the ruins of Ur seem to show that commercial
relations between Chaldea and south India existed from at
least the 8th century before Christ, and it is probable that
the Sumerian founders of Babylonia were themselves of
Dravidian stock. Roman coins of the reigns of Tiberius and
Nero have been discovered in Malabar, and, as we have
seen, St. Bartholomew may well have preached the gospel
in these parts. The division of the native Christians of
Malabar into two distinct castes—Suddists [20] and Nordists,[21]
a condition of affairs which still exists, might lend colour
to the theory of this twofold apostolate. An altogether
baseless legend says that in 345 Thomas of Cana (or even
St. Thomas) had two wives with two establishments at
Cranganore, the one on the north bank of the river and the

[19] Root *saba*, " to make a trading journey;" cf. Sheba.
[20] Malayalam, *Thekumpavur*, " of the South country."
[21] Malayalam, *Vatakumpavur*, " of the North country."

other on the south, and that the two castes are the descendents of the respective wives! A Suddist is certainly
called *Knanaya,* but the connection of the term with Cana
is etymologically impossible, as the Syrian adjective in that
case would be *Knanoito.* The word points rather to Kane
near Aden, suggesting that the Suddists are the descendents
of the original Jewish colony in Malabar, who may have had
St. Bartholomew as their apostle. This caste, as it later became, was ostracised as an alien community when the tho-
roughly Indianised Pehlevi Christians (Nordists) arrived from
the north of the country. The Nordists, representing the rul-
ing power, claimed to be the children of St. Thomas, and
the Suddists were compelled to exchange Bar Tolmai for
Mar Thoma as the apostle of the country. St. Thomas
can at least be honoured as the bearer of the gospel to
India, and his feast, July 3, is kept as a holiday of obligation.
Local tradition ascribes the composition of the office for
that day to Indian prelates of the 1st or 2nd century. The
blessings which India has received as a result of the apostolate of St. Thomas are described in detail: "Through
Mar Thoma a splendid mansion was built for India in
the heights of heaven. Through Mar Thoma the kings
of India longed to be happy in it. Through Mar Thoma
all the Indians attached themselves to truth and renounc-
ed error. Through Mar Thoma they (Indians) took up
the spiritual weapon of baptism. Through Mar Thoma
the country of India was washed from her stains. Through
Mar Thoma the seed of life sprouted in India, instead of
weeds. Through Mar Thoma India bore the sweet fruits
of the spirit. Through Mar Thoma she (India) submitted
to the sweet yoke of Christ. Through Mar Thoma churches
and sanctuaries were constructed throughout India, in which
prayers and praises are offered to Christ the King."

The early history of Christianity in Malabar remains obscure, and John the Persian, who at the first council of Nicea (325) described himself as "over the churches in all Persia and Great India," [22] was probably a Syrian bishop, who claimed jurisdiction in India. There seems little doubt that the faith was received in Malabar from East Syria, with the liturgy, rites and ceremonies of that church. St. Ephrem speaks of a flourishing Christianity in India, with a fully developed cultus of St. Thomas; while, as we have seen, the numbers of the faithful were augmented by refugees from the Persian persecution.

Local tradition ranks Thomas of Cana high among these voluntary exiles, and he is alleged to have come to the country accompanied by about five hundred families, a bishop (Mar Joseph), and many priests and deacons. An Indian king [23] is said to have granted great privileges to the immigrants, and Thomas of Cana is looked upon by the Malabarese as the second founder of their church.

The favours that were thus conceded were inscribed on a copper-plate in Karmataka (ancient Indian language), with signatures in Arabic and Syriac, but the original seems to have been lost some time after 1544. Assemani [24] and Diego de Conto, [25] however, think that the story belongs to the 9th century rather than to the 4th.

[22] Some ancient West Syrian writers have thought that "Great India" was Ethiopia and Arabia Felix.
[23] Malabar tradition speaks of Cheraman Perumal; while a Portuguese manuscript volume in the British Museum, dated 1604, gives Cocurangon. Leclercq (*Dict. d'Archéol. Chrét.* etc. IX, col. 1260) mentions Cheraman Perumal, pagan king of Malabar, who accorded many privileges to the Christians of his kingdom. The growth of the church, continues the learned Benedictine, led to the accession of Baliartes, who was known as the "King of the Christians of St. Thomas."

About the year 354, Theophilus the Indian was sent by the emperor Constantinus to his native country, an event recorded by the Arian Philostorgius: [26] "Thence (from the Maldives) he sailed to other parts of India, and reformed many things which were not rightly done among them; for they heard the reading of the gospel in a sitting posture, and did other things which were repugnant to the divine law; and having reformed everything according to the holy usage, as was most acceptable to God, he also confirmed the dogma of the church."

The traveller Cosmas Indicopleustes [27] in the 6th century (530-535) speaks of Christians in Malabar under Persian jurisdiction; while about the same time a Jacobite monk, Bud (Ba'uth) Periodeutes, says that he found Christians in India.

The Edessene scholar Mana, bishop of Riwardashir (ab. 470), who wrote sermons, canticles and hymns in Pahlevi, and translated the works of Diodore and Theodore of Mopsuestia from Greek into Syriac, sending his literary efforts to "India," may very well have been instructing his Malankara co-religionists in their religion.

It seems indeed certain that the early church of Malabar depended on that of East Syria in much the same way as Ethiopia depended on Egypt, with a single bishop, who had no suffragans, consecrated by the patriarch of the mother church. In 857, the Nestorian patriarch Theodosius I (852-858) included India among those countries, which by reason

[24] *Bibl. Orient.*, III, part. II, pp. 443-444.
[25] *Decada* XII.
[26] See PHOTIUS, *Bibliotheca.*
[27] *Topographia.*

of their great distance [28] should send letters of communion only once in six years. How far did this submission to a church which was at least materially heretical involve the Malabarese? The Portuguese, after at first treating them as fellow Catholics, accused them of Nestorianism, and the treatment meeted out by the Western power makes sad reading. The history of this period, however, and the defence of the native Christians against the charge of heresy will be considered later in the chapter.

In 880, two brothers, Mar Sapor and Mar Prodh, came to Malabar, where they preached the gospel and worked miracles. Christianity, says Le Quien, [29] was very flourishing at this time in the kingdom of Diamper, and the whole church of Malabar honoured their names. Later, they came to be regarded as saints (*kadisae*), and churches were erected in their honour at Diamper and Quilon. The latter was built in 925, if the "Report" is correct in saying that it was one hundred years after the foundation of the town. The missionaries, having come from "Babylon," were therefore suspect to the Portuguese, and the synod of Diamper [30] (1599) ordered that their churches should in future be dedicated in honour of All Saints, for "since they came from Babylon there is just cause to suspect they might be heretics."

In 883, Sighelm (Suithelm), bishop of Sherborne, and Aethelstan were sent to Malabar on the instructions [31] of

[28] This regulation may be compared with the Cistercian annual general chapter, which, as the order spread into distant lands, granted dispensations for abbots to come to Citeaux only every fourth, fifth or even seventh year.

[29] *Oriens Christianus*, t. II, col. 1275.

[30] Decree XXV, session VIII.

[31] "And that same year (883) Sighelm and Aethelstan carried to Rome the alms which the king had vowed to send thither, and also to

King Alfred of Wessex (871-901), who, when the Danes
were besieging London, had made a vow that if he was
victorious he would send an embassage to Rome and to the
"Church of the Apostles Bartholomew and Thomas."

Monumental evidence for Christianity in India is found
in a mural inscription (Pali) in a celebrated pagoda at Udai-
pur, Malwa (central India), which is believed to have been
formerly a Christian church dedicated in honour of our
Lady. Sangai Vardaha (Lion the Generous), king of the
Saces, rebuilt the edifice about the year 1060, and the inscription speaks of the blessed Virgin as the Mother of God,
and recognises the supremacy of the pope: "... having gone
through all the exterior rites and received with one eager
care the sublime instructions of the priest, they may partake
of the glory of the life which descends upon the sacred altar.
That the suffering souls may be delivered from their tor-
ments and receive their portion of the celestial happiness.
And also to know the saints who have triumphed... The
time soon arrived when he who works wonders incompre-
hensible in the heart of man was to come down from heaven
in order to rise from the oblations, being born once more in
answer to our prayers. And, the Consecration finished
(*Nittar Maittam*) he, who is in the heaven of heavens, is

India, to St. Thomas and to St. Bartholomew, when they sat down
against the army at London; and there, thanks be to God, they largely
obtained the object of their prayer after the vow." *Anglo-Saxon Chronicle;* ap. *Church Historians of England*, vol. II, part I, p. 48, Seeleys,
Fleet Street and Hanover Street, 1853.

"And sent many presents over sea to Rome and to St. Thomas in
India. Sighelm, bishop of Sherborne, sent as ambassador for this purpose,
penetrated successfully into India, a matter of astonishment even in the
present time. Returning thence, he brought back many brilliant exotic
gems and aromatic juices in which that country abounds." William of
MALMESBURY, *Chronicle of the Kings of England*, book II, chap. IV,
p. 118. (Giles) London, George Bell, 1904.

there, offering himself with his real body and soul, with his sovereign and divine nature... the divine master, becoming bread, gives himself up.   But through the effect of an order superior to that of nature, though divided and eaten, it preserves its integrity and incorruptibility... But he who directs and conducts its execution, the most merciful heir and lord of the whole earth (*parvini juxta*), the head of the priesthood (*tadaj-jajar*, i. e. the pope), Victor, sent a relic, this will surely be for our church a means of victory and welfare, since it proceeds from the chief of our Mother (?Church)."   It is not known when Christianity was extinguished in the district of Malwa, but there can be little doubt as to its orthodoxy at the time when the inscription was written.

The Middle Ages

Representatives of the Nestorian church were sent to Malabar in 998 (Mar John) and again in 1056 (Mar Thomas); while in 1122 John III, [32] "archbishop of India" and self-styled "patriarch," went with his suffragans, by way of Constantinople, to Rome.   Here they were received by Pope Calixtus II (1119-1124), who, on hearing of the miracles performed by St. Thomas at Mylapore, invested John with the pallium.   The Venetian traveller, Marco Polo (ab. 1254-1324), on his return from China, described the "pepper coast of Malabar" and the tomb of the great apostle, but he gave no account of the Christian community,

[32] It has been suggested by those who maintain that the church of Malabar was Catholic until at least the 12th century that John had been sent to India by the patriarch of Antioch. *De Fontibus Juris Ecclesiastici Syro-Malankarensium. Fonti.* Serie II, Fascicolo VIII. P. a S. Joseph, p. 21.

beyond the fact that the shrine of St. Thomas was venerated by Christians and Moslems alike: "The Christians who go in pilgrimage take of the earth of the place where the saint was killed (a custom still practised) and give a portion thereof to any who is sick, and by the power of God and of St. Thomas the sick man is incontinently cured."

John of Montecorvino, [33] a Franciscan missionary, was sent in 1291 by Pope Nicholas IV to preach the faith in Asia. After a short sojourn in Persia, he went, by way of the Indian ports, to China, where he arrived in 1294 and stayed until his death in 1329. Writing from Cambales (Pekin) in 1305 and 1306, the intrepid Franciscan said that he stayed thirteen months in that part of India where the church of St. Thomas stood (Mylapore), baptizing about a hundred persons, and that there were in Malabar a few Christians and Jews who were of little worth, only "the inhabitants persecute much the Christians and all who bear the Christian name."

In 1321, a Dominican named Jordan came to India, returning to Avignon for consecration as Latin bishop of Quilon, at the hands of Pope John XXII (1314-1334). He returned to his diocese in 1330, armed with two papal letters. The first of these, addressed to the "Chief [34] of the Christians of Quilon," directed "that divisions cease and clouds of error stain not the brightness of the faith of all regenerated by the waters of baptism... and that the phantom of schism and wilful blindness towards the holy faith darken not the vision of those who believe in Christ and adore his name."

The second, which was for the Christians at Moleph-

[33] *Yule. Cathay and the Way Thither*, I.
[34] "*Nobili vivo domino Nascarinorum et universis sub es Christianis Nascarinis de Columbo...*"

atam (Gulf of Manaar), was similar in tone, and stressed the importance of union with the Roman church. About 1324, Malabar was visited by another Franciscan missionary on his way to China, Blessed Odoric of Pordenone; while in 1348 Pope Clement VI (1342-1352) sent a legate, in the person of John de Marignoli, a Franciscan bishop. This legate, who spoke of Mylapore as Mirapolis, said of his visit: " Nor are the Saracens the proprietors of pepper, but the Christians of St. Thomas. And these latter are the masters of the public weighing-office, from which I derived as a perquisite of my office as pope's legate, every month, a hundred gold fanams and a thousand when I left... So after one year and four months I took leave of the brethren." Pope Eugenius IV (1431-1447) in 1439 sent a letter to the reigning prince in Malabar with the following dedication: "To my most beloved son in Christ, Thomas, the illustrious Emperor of the Indians, Health and Apostolic Benediction. There has often reached us a constant rumour that your Serenity and all who are subjects of your kingdom are *true* Christians." The pope certainly does not seem to have thought that the Indian Church was suspect of Nestorianism, although distance often made it difficult to ascertain the true facts. The Christian royal house, [35] after ten centuries, appears to have become extinct [36] at about the end of the 15th century, and the country came under the rule of the pagan king of Cochin.

[35] Villalvetta dynasty, called in Portuguese and Dutch writings *Baliarte*.
[36] In the early years of the 16th century, a palace of Christian kings existed at Udayamperur in north Travancore.

The Coming of the Portuguese

Thus matters stood until 1498, when the Portuguese navigator, Vasco da Gama, landed in Malabar. The Christian families were said to number thirty thousand, and in 1502, on the second voyage, the explorer was given the sceptre of the last Christian king of Cochin, a red rod tipped with silver and ornamented at the top with three small bells. Vasco da Gama in return promised "protection" to the people in the name of his king, Emmanuel I (1495-1521). The term "protection" had already come to mean conquest rather than kindly assistance in time of difficulty!

The presence of an ever growing body of Latin Catholics in Malabar soon raised the question as to the orthodoxy of the " church of the country." Many of the Portuguese were as much concerned with the propagation and extension of the faith as with material gain in respect to wealth and commerce.

Here was a liturgy celebrated in an unknown tongue with unaccustomed rites and ceremonies: what were to be the reactions of the Portuguese? Were the native Christians of Malabar Nestorian in doctrine or was their Christology orthodox?

These were some of the questions which had to be answered, more especially after the establishment of a Latin hierarchy.

In 1501, Joseph the Indian [37] had written to Pope Alexander VI, maintaining that his katholikos was subject to the pope, but the commonly accepted view of Western Catholics, at least until recently, has been that the church of Malabar

---

[37] RAULIN, *Historia Ecclesiae Malabaricae*, p. 386.

was rescued from Nestorianism by the Portuguese in the
16th century. The Indians themselves, however, have
maintained that their ancestors were never Nestorian, and
that the calumny was invented in order to further a policy
of latinization. Thus, in two adresses [38] presented in 1887
to Mgr, later Cardinal, Ajuti, the Malabarese clergy declare:
"Though it is assumed by the Portuguese that they converted our forefathers from the Nestorian heresy and restored
them to the union of the holy Catholic Church, yet we offer
our grateful homage to the Almighty for having kept us
away as a body from all heresies, and preserved us in the
union of the holy Catholic Church from the time of the
Apostle Thomas."

A *Padiola* document, taken from the archives of the
Mannanam monastery, embodies an oath which was taken
by Catholics and schismatics alike on June 20, 1799, at the
Church of the Holy Cross, Alleppy, with a view to the ter-
mination of the schism. The belief that the church of Malabar never ceased to be in communion with the Apostolic
See is expressed in the clearest terms: "From the time of
our ancient forefathers till the year 1599 we were observing
the Syro-Chaldean rite *of those who were in communion
with the holy Roman Church;* but owing to the interruption
of the Syrian bishops *who are in communion with Rome* (by
the intervention of the Portuguese in India) we were deprived of episcopal dignities. Then Dom Alexis Menezes,
archbishop of Goa, ... arrived in Malabar and convoked a
synod at Diamper." This is the claim of the Malankara
church, is there any evidence forthcoming to substantiate it?

Some supporters of continuous orthodoxy assert that a

[38] August 31, 1887, at Mannanam; September 15, 1887, at
Ampalachat.

remnant of the East Syrians remained faithful to Ephesus (431), perpetuating a secret hierarchy, and that it was only with this little flock that the church of south India maintained communion. In defence of this theory, it is said that the Nestorian patriarch, Abraham II, about the year 1000, sent a complaint to the kaliph of Bagdad, that a katholikos, subject to the patriarch of Antioch, was consecrating bishop by night, and as a result of the charge the offending prelates were imprisoned. Peter, patriarch (Byzantine) of Antioch, writing to Dominic of Grado (ab. 1050), claims that his jurisdiction extends to the far east, including India, and that he appoints katholikoi for Babylon and other regions, who in their turn have bishops subject to them. It is suggested therefore that Malabar obtained bishops from that source, and that these katholikoi, after the schism of 1053, maintained direct communication with Rome. Centuries before these alleged happenings, however, Persia had severed her connection with the Seleucian primate, and the patriarch, Jesu-Yab III [39] (650-661), had complained to Simon of Yakut (Riwardashir): "In your own country, from the time you have revolted from the canons of the Church, the succession of priesthood has been cut off from the people of India, nor from India alone... but also your own country of Persia lies in darkness, deprived of the light of divine doctrine which shines forth through bishops of the truth." In the following century, says the Monophysite writer, Bar Hebraeus, the Persian metropolitan told Timothy, the Nestorian patriarch (778-823): "We are the disciples of Thomas the Apostle, and have nothing to do with the see of Mari." This resulted in the removal of Malabar from the supervision of Persia, which seems to

[39] Joseph ASSEMANI, *Bibliotheca Orientalis*, l. VIII, p. 27.

28 - A. A. KING, *The Rites of Eastern Christendom* - 2nd Vol.

[17]

point to the fact that, at least in the 8th century, south India was under Nestorian jurisdiction. The Malabarese, however, assert that their church now severed all inter-communion with the East Syrians, and support the claim by showing that so early as 774 their bishop had the titles of "Metropolitan" and Gate of all India," retaining the last named until the end of the 18th century. The evidence would hardly justify the assertion that the church of Malabar never tolerated any *communicatio cum haereticis,* but there is not the slightest proof that it was ever formally Nestorian. The Indians do not seem to have indulged in any Christological speculations, and to have been as ready to obtain bishops from Jacobite sources as from Nestorian, not only in the 17th century, but as early as the 7th. The Copts, it appears, were applied to for a bishop in the time of the patriarch Isaac (686-689), and, when the negotiations were unsuccessful, a West Syrian bishop was appointed in Malabar (696).

The Portuguese, for the first fifty years after their arrival, seem to have had no doubts regarding the orthodoxy of the native Christians. St. Francis Xavier visited the country on his way to the far East, and met Jacob (Jacome Abuna), one of the four bishops [40] who came to Malabar in 1504, and in his letter [41] to King John III of Portugal (1521-1551) the saint speaks of the interview without any suggestion of a conversion or reconciliation. The bishop had served God in Malabar for forty-five years, and "now in his all but decrepit old age he conforms himself most obediently to all the rites and customs of our holy mother the Roman Church." A letter, written to the Society of

[40] Thomas, Jaballa, Deneha, Jacob.
[41] Written from Cochin, January 26, 1549.

Jesus in Rome on September 18, 1542, speaks of the unsatisfactory state of religion in the island of Socotra, but St. Francis points out that the Christians there give special honour to the Apostle Thomas, claiming to be the "descendents of Christians begotten to Jesus Christ by that apostle." When, however, in 1680 the Carmelite Vincenzo Maria di Santa Caterina visited the island Christianity was all but extinct. St. Francis, in speaking of the Malabarese, often adopts a Portuguese name for them, "Armenians," that is *Aramaensor* or Syrians. Writing in February 1548 to the Jesuit fathers on the Comorin coast the great missionary said: "You will be very kind to the Malabar priests and provide for their good with all consideration, especially in matters belonging to religion, taking care that they accustom themselves to go regularly to confession, that they offer the holy Sacrifice with all propriety and very often, and that they set a right example of holy living to the people." Finally, in respect to the evidence afforded by St. Francis Xavier as to Malabarese orthodoxy, we may quote a letter written to St. Ignatius Loyola (January 14,1549), in which he speaks of these native Christians in much the same way as he would of any Catholic people: "Fr. Vincenzo [42] has founded a really fine seminary where quite as many as one hundred native students are maintained and formed in piety and learning... He has asked me again and again to provide a priest of the Society, who may teach grammar to the students of the seminary, and preach to the inmates and the people on Sundays and festivals. There is reason for this because, besides the Portuguese inhabitants of the place, there are a great many Christians living in sixty villages in the neighbourhood, descended from those whom St. Tho-

---

[42] A Franciscan who was sent to Malabar in 1530.

mas made Christians. The students of the seminary are of
the higher nobility. In this town there are two churches,
one of St. Thomas and one of St. James. Fr. Vincenzo...
hopes much that you get each of them a plenary indulgence
once a year from the Holy Father, on the feasts of St. Thomas and St. James and the seven days after each. This
would *increase the piety of the natives,* who are descended
from the converts of St. Thomas and are generally called
the "Christians of St. Thomas." Much the same was said
by St. Francis fourteen days later, in a letter to Fr. Simon
Rodriguez: "There is a fine college here (Cranganore),
which was built by Fr. Vincenzo, the companion of the
bishop, where as many as a hundred youths, children of the
native Christians, who are called the "Christians of St. Thomas," are educated... At Cranganore there are two churches,
one of St. Thomas and another of St. James adjoining the
college. Fr. Vincenzo wishes very much that an indulgence
should be obtained for both these churches, to be a con-
solation for these Christians and *to increase their piety*...
I would have this indulgence offered only to those *who have
duly approached the sacraments of Penance and Holy Communion* and then piously and devotedly visited these churches at Cranganore."

Portuguese testimony, also, is not wanting to show that
it was only in the *second* half of the 16th century that the
Malabarese were accused of Nestorianism. Thus, Ludovico
da Varthema in his *Travels* (1505) said: "They believe in
Christ *as we do*... In this city (Quilon) we found some
Christians of those of St. Thomas, some of whom are mer-
chants and they believe in Christ *as we do*... These Christians keep Lent longer than we do, but they keep Easter
like ourselves and they all observe the same solemnities as
we do. But they say the Mass like the Greeks."

The Portuguese, in the early days of colonisation, treated the native Christians in all respects as co-religionists, hearing their confessions, giving them holy communion and lending churches for the celebrations of the Syrian liturgy; while provincial synods enacted decrees in regard to the oriental rite. Contemporary Portuguese writers are quite clear on this point, and the Jesuit, Fr. Maffei, spoke of the Malabarese as the "faithful [43] of Christ that still existed in that country."

The four East Syrian bishops, [44] who, in response to the petition sent in 1490 to the Nestorian patriarch, arrived in Malabar in 1504, despatched a long report [45] to the katholikos, in which they remarked on the brotherly welcome that they had received from the Portuguese: "There are here thirty thousand families common in faith [46] with us and they pray God for your prosperity. Our province in which the Christians dwell is called Malabar and has about twenty cities. In all these, Christians dwell and churches have been built. About twenty Portuguese live in the city of Cannanore. When we arrived from Ormuz at Cannanore we presented ourselves to them, said that we were Christians and *explained our condition and rank. They received us with great joy...* We remained with them for two and a half months and they ordered us that on a fixed day we also should celebrate the holy mysteries (should offer the obla-

---

[43] "Ut Christi fideles quotquot in ea regione supersint."

[44] Portuguese writers mention only two bishops in the early years of their colonisation, John, who had come to the country before their arrival, and Jacob, the friend of St. Francis Xavier.

[45] The document, together with a Latin translation, is in the Vatican archives. GIAMIL, *Genuinae Relationes inter Sedem Apostolicam et Chaldaeorum Ecclesiam*, pp. 594-596, Rome, 1902.

[46] This might be taken to imply that the church of Malabar was Nestorian, but, as we have seen, the East Syrian church, despite its support of Nestorius and other heretics, never formally embraced heresy.

tion). They had prepared a proper place for prayer, which they called the oratory and their priests offer sacrifice every day...; for that is their custom and rite. Whereof on Nusardel Sunday (first Sunday "of Summer"), after their priests had celebrated, we also were admitted and offered the holy Sacrifice, and it was very pleasing in their eyes."

In reference to the coming of the Portuguese to India, the same bishops also said: "Know this also, fathers, namely that powerful ships were sent from the west to this land of the Indies by the king of the Christians *who are our brethren (ähäin)*, the Portuguese (*Prängäye*)... The rest... came to our Christians at Cochin, with whom they entered into brotherly relations" (*asel lkäreevootä*).

The opposition to the native church and accusations of heresy seem primarily to have come after the establishment of the diocese of Goa.

This see was erected in 1534 as a suffragan to Funchal in the Madeiras, and was made an independent archbishopric in 1557. Historians [47] of the synod of Diamper (1599) and of the church of Malabar have all been beholden to Antonio de Gouvea, a Portuguese Augustinian hermit, who, writing under the influence of Alexius de Menezes,[48] archbishop of Goa (1559-1617) and a member of the same order, produced in his *Jornada* [49] an altogether *ex parte* and unreliable account of the facts.

---

[47] e. g. Geddes, La Croze, Assemani, Raulin, Le Quien, Hough.

[48] In spite, however, of the evident prejudices of the archbishop, Menezes had said in 1599: "*Vehementer nos commovebat commiseratio gentis illius* (in the original text: *commovidos tamben de piedade desta gente*), *cuius magna pars a tempore quo ipsi S. Apostolus Thomas Evangelium promulgaverat, ad haec usque tempora in Christi Domini fide constans perseverabat.*" De Fontibus Juris Ecclesiastici Syro-Malankarensium, serie II, fascic. VIII, p. 38.

[49] *Jornada do Arcebispo Aleixo de Menezes foy as Serras do Ma-*

The Malabarese and even their hieratic tongue (Syro-Chaldean) came to be called, without the slightest justification, Nestorian. Thus, Fr. Wrede [50] says that "these Christians are indiscriminately called St. Thomas Christians, Nestorians, Syrians, and sometimes the Malabar Christians of the mountains (Serra) by the Portuguese writers and by the subsequent missionaries from Rome." Mr. Mackenzie, [51] a former British resident in Travancore and Cochin, wrote: "It must be conceded that the epithet "Nestorian" is loosely used by the Portuguese writers and sometimes denotes a member of the Oriental Church without connoting any idea of heresy."

The two last bishops of the old Syrian hierarchy, Mar Joseph Sulaka and Mar Abraham, came to Malabar after the Portuguese had arrived in the country. It was with them that the smouldering fires of Latin distrust burst into flame, and therefore it is of importance to ascertain whether there was any ground for suspecting their orthodoxy. Mar Joseph was a brother of John Sulaka, who had been nominated Chaldean patriarch by Pope Julius III (1549-1555) with jurisdiction "in Sin Massin et Calicuth et tota India"; while his successor, Ebed Jesu, had sent him to Malabar. The bishop arrived in India with letters from the pope [52] to the Portuguese authorities, and accompanied by Mgr. Ambrose, [53] a Dominican prelate and papal commissary to

---

lauvar. Coimbras 1606. Gouvea himself was in Malabar from the year 1591 till 1602.

[50] Asiatic Researches, vol. VII, p. 362.

[51] Travancore State Manual, vol. II, 157.

[52] Pope Julius III in the bull Divina disponente clementia (1553) had recognised and confirmed the jurisdiction of the Chaldean patriarch in Malabar.

[53] Mgr. Ambrose died at Cochin.

the first Catholic patriarch, his *socius* Fr. Antony, and Mar Hormisdas, archbishop of Diarberkir. They came about the year 1563 to Goa, where Mar Joseph [54] was detained for eighteen months, although he was at first the subject of praise, since he had brought order, decorum and propriety into the church services, as well as introduced azyme bread and Roman vestments. The latinising policy, however, does not seem to have been carried out on his own volition, and, when asked by the Chaldean patriarch for an explanation, the bishop excused himself on the plea that his position was that of "an anvil under the hammer."

Friction arose ostensibly from the refusal of Mar Joseph to ordain students from Cranganore who were ignorant of Syriac, but there seems little doubt that his presence in Malabar was distasteful to the Portuguese from the very first.

The Chaldean patriarch obtained leave from the pope for visitors, who were not Portuguese, in order that they might make a report on the conditions prevailing in the country. The archbishop of Diarbekir, in a letter to Cardinal Caraffa, the protector of the Chaldean church, requested his eminence to obtain an order from Rome forbidding the practice of calling the Syro-Chaldeans "Nestorians:" "We beg therefore that your eminence may again

---

[54] "From this year 1558 there governed the Christians of St. Thomas one Mar Joseph with the title of archbishop, and this archbishop, in order to show himself a Catholic and to gain the good will of the Portuguese, put the affairs of the Serra into better order so far as concerns the Mass and Divine Office. He introduced vestments in the Roman style, for before that they had celebrated covered with an amice and over that a stole. He gave orders to use our hosts and our wine, for before that they had consecrated lumps (*bolos*) kneaded with oil and salt and sweet wine (*mosto*), squeezed from moistened raisins." *Oriente Conquistado*, I, 86; ap. MACKENZIE, *Christianity in Travancore*, p. 65.

obtain for this people the favour already in the past obtained that they may not be called Nestorians, but Eastern Chaldeans... and that this may be published to the whole world and to all countries."

Finally, Mar Joseph was accused to the bishop of Cochin of having reverted to Nestorianism. It was alleged that he took some youths apart and told them that although they might venerate the blessed Virgin as the refuge of sinners and the Mother of Christ, that it was strictly forbidden to call her the Mother of God.

Mar Joseph was sent to Portugal, in order that he might from thence submit his case to the pope in person, and he obtained the goodwill of the queen, who, after he had made a profession of faith before Cardinal Henry, sent him back to Malabar. Gouvea says that he again caused scandal by his heterodox opinions, and the Portuguese cardinal reported the matter to Pope St. Pius V (1567-1572), who sent a brief (January 15, 1567) to George, archbishop of Goa, ordering him to make the fullest enquiry. The first provincial council of Goa held the charges against Mar Joseph to be substantiated, and in 1568 the unfortunate prelate was again deported to Portugal, from whence he continued his journey to Rome. He died soon after arrival, and, according to the Malabarese, on the very day before he was to receive the sacred purple, so that suspicion of foul play was alleged, although the Portuguese maintained that he was still in disgrace. The reception in Malabar of the other bishop, Mar Abraham, was no better than that of his predecessor, but his early career appears to have been somewhat equivocal. He was first sent to India by the Nestorian patriarch Simon, where he was acclaimed by the people, and officiated at episcopal ceremonies.

Then exiled to Portugal, Mar Abraham escaped at Mozambique and returned to Mesopotamia, where he was nominated and consecrated a Catholic bishop by Ebed Jesu, the Chaldean patriarch, who gave him a letter of commendation to the pope. Arrived in Rome, Mar Abraham made a profession of faith and a declaration as to the validity of his orders, but he was none the less obliged to receive them again from the tonsure to the priesthood, at the hands of the bishop of San Severino. The profession of faith was similar to that which he made in later years to Pope Gregory XIII (1572-1585): " ... with a firm faith believe and profess each and everything contained in the symbol of faith that the holy Roman Church makes use of. So I believe in one God (continues in the words of the Creed at Mass) .... I acknowledge the Chatholic Apostolic and Roman Church as the mother and mistress of all churches. I profess and swear true obedience to the Roman Pontiff, the successor of blessed Peter, the prince of the apostles, the vicar of Jesus Christ." Finally, in virtue of a papal brief, Mar Abraham was consecrated archbishop of Angamaly by the patriarch of Venice. Thus equipped, the "much ordained" prelate returned to Malabar with letters of commendation to the archbishop of Goa and the bishop of Cochin. Pope Pius IV (1559-1565), in a letter to the Latin metropolitan dated February 28, 1565, had written: "Our beloved brother Abraham of the Chaldean nation, consecrated, as we hear, bishop in that diocese ... his great and remarkable devotion to the Apostolic See touched us in particular. Despite we had already known him to be a religious and pious man from the valuable testimonies of his patriarch *and of all those that are well acquainted with him* in those parts."

Then recounting the eulogies given by Mar Ebed Jesu, the pope continued: "for since he has so diligently written of him, care must be taken lest he should have any just cause of complaint, which would be the case if what he has judged about this be neglected."

The same day, also, the letter was written to the bishop of Cochin, in which the pope declared that so long as Mar Abraham persevered in the Catholic faith he was to be maintained and defended in his diocese: "After his (Ebed Jesu) model Abraham also professed his faith to the Holy See and promised in a document, subscribed by his own hand, that he would profess the true faith for ever and would transmit the same to those over whom he was placed .... He is to be embraced by you with fraternal charity, regarding his communion with the Holy See, and also out of consideration for his patriarch, and that while he perseveres in faith and in his obedience to the Holy See he is to be defended from all injury that, protected by your patronage, without any molestation and impediment he may be *able to remain where his patriarch placed him* .... Wherefore take care that you diligently protect him from all injury in such a way that he may understand how much you regard us and the Holy See and how much you love the equality and justice of the same see. For we wish and desire him to hold without any impediment that diocese which his patriarch assigned to him." Five days earlier (February 23, 1565), the pope had written to the Chaldean patriarch about the sorely tried bishop: "He could by his own name recommend himself to us and could kindly be received by us .... a good fosterer of sacred letters and Catholic dogma according to the information we have of him .... We are grieved at the inconveniences he suffered in India .... On his return to India we gave him letters of recommendation at your request. But we think it expedient that your fraternity assign him a diocese and a place of residence, and to divide the diocese between him and the other bishop (Mar Joseph) of your nationality .... also exert as much as you can (as you have promised you would do) that the faith of those over whom you are placed may entirely agree with the faith of the holy Roman Catholic Apostolic Church, and that it might not disagree in anything, which of course is necessary for salvation. For, as regards rites and ceremonies (and it would be very decent), although it is to be desired that they too agree, still we would permit you to retain the customs and the old rites, which of course can be proved (to be legitimate), provided in sacraments and other things pertaining to faith and necessary for salvation you follow, as we said, the Roman Church, the *Mater et Magistra* of all Christians. We recommend our nuncio to your charity. Most beloved brother, may the Almighty God protect you safe, together with your clergy and people." The above letters are preserved in the Vatican archives, and they were published in 1902 by Samuel Giamel, procurator of the Chaldean patriarch, under the title *Genuinae Relationes inter Sedem Apostolicam et Chaldaeorum Ecclesiam*.

Mar Abraham, however, in spite of the express approbation of the pope, was not welcomed by the Portuguese ecclesiastical authorities. On his arrival in Goa, he was interned in a religious house, but he escaped to Malabar, where his work was continually hindered by accusations of heresy. The pagan king of Cochin seems to have taken up his cause, and on January 2, 1576, he wrote on behalf of the persecuted bishop to Pope Gregory XIII: "Mar Abraham, archbishop of Angamaly .... could not, as he was requested, be present at the provincial council convoked by the archbishop of Goa on account of the wrongs and oppressions done towards him, and also because he was twice committed to prison. So he could not sit in the said council, and he has asked me to inform your holiness that *he remains an obedient son to the holy Apostolic See,* and that if your holiness will assure him, he will be present at the conucil of these states and will communicate with Portuguese prelates and religious to the great utility of Christianity. His archdeacon George of Christ has requested me to obtain for him from your holiness certain indulgences for a church he has newly built in honour of the Assumption, which feast is celebrated in the month of August."

The pope, in answer to this letter, wrote (November 28, 1578) to the archbishop of Goa: "We wish that in the provincial synod you receive the archbishop of Angamaly." A petition in 1578 was sent to Rome by some of the leading native Christians, and signed by three of the *rais banda,* [55] in which the pope was begged to ask the Chaldean patriarch that he might, according to the ancient custom, send them five bishops: "To our most holy father and lord the pope, great pastor of those of Christ ..... that we are ..... partakers of sacraments and the body of our Lord God; and that our liturgical prayers are in the Syriac (Chaldaic) language transmitted to us by our Father St. Thomas ..... Mar Elias left us orphans and went away .... Wherefore our Father Ebediesus for the love of Christ had sent us the metropolitan bishop, Mar Abraham, with his own letters and the letters of our father and lord the most holy pope; we heard that when he came to the blessed city of Goa he was detained by the viceroy. .... Thou art the father of all Christians and therefore deign to do with thy flock as it becomes thy kingdom and fare thou well in the Lord."

Persecution and misrepresentation, however, never seem to have affected the loyalty of Mar Abraham, and the pope

[55] "Head of a town," " prefect of a station." Syriac, *resa,* "head" or " chief," *bandar,* " bazaar."

on November 29, 1578, wrote to him: "The letter of your fraternity was very pleasing to us. For it was full of love and regard in recognising the authority of the Apostolic See and *in testifying your Catholic faith.*" Fr. Monserrato, a Spanish Jesuit, suggested, in the following year, to the general of the Society of Jesus that the pope would do well to send a nuncio to Malabar who was not Portuguese, but the sound advice went unheeded. On March 5,1580, Pope Gregory XIII sent a warning to the clergy and people of Malabar against a heretic named Simeon, who claimed to be in episcopal orders, at the same time encouraging them in their support of Mar Abraham: "to have tried to seduce the Catholics from the unity of the Church, to corrupt the Orthodox faith and to disseminate his false doctrines..... Be ye therefore obedient to your lord archbishop Abraham and also to George, the bishop of Palur, and live stedfast in the sincerity of faith." In point of fact, George, a native of Koravilangad (Travancore), was only an archdeacon, but with the approval of Rome he had been nominated bishop by the Chaldean patriarch, Simon Denha (1580-1600), and the pope was under the impression that he had been already consecrated. In 1583, at the instance of the local superior of the Society of Jesus, Fr. Valignano, a synod was held for the church of Malabar at Angamaly, and once again the clergy made a profession of faith, which the Portuguese authorities now called the "first reconciliation of the Syrians to the Church!"

Mar Abraham in the following year (January 13,1584) sent yet another expression of filial submission to the pope: "Most beloved and holy father, lying prostrate at your holiness' most blessed feet and craving the paternal blessing, we have written this letter as a testimony of our bounden obedience... We find ourselves bound by the greatest bond

of obligation towards your Holiness." A further petition
to the pope, probably sent by members of the Society
of Jesus, speaks of "the reduction of the Christians of
St. Thomas to the obedience and to the rites (sic) of the
holy Roman Church." The pope is begged to see that Mar
Abraham and Archdeacon George are duly recognised and
well treated by the Portuguese. "Moreover," the petition
continues, "we beg that your holiness would grant for a
church which the said archbishop has newly built at Angamaly, under the invocation of St. Hormisdas or St. Hormas
(the abbot through whom our Lord works many miracles),
a plenary indulgence on the days when the feast of the said
saint is celebrated, which are two every year."

In 1585, Mar Abraham was present at the third session
of the provincial synod of Goa, when ten decrees [56] affecting
the church of Malabar were promulgated. The fifth canon
forbade the ordination [57] of Syrians by foreign bishops
without the permission of the ordinary; required the
appointment to a Church to be in the hands of the Latin
authorities; and newly ordained priests were ordered to
celebrate the Latin Mass in Latin Churches and the Syrian
Mass in Syrian churches.

The sixth canon repeated the first canon of the synod
of 1575 (sixth session): Malabarese bishops must be
appointed by the king of Portugal, and consecrated at Goa.

The seventh ordered the translation of the Roman ritual
and pontifical for use in the diocese of Angamaly; while the

[56] The synod of 1585 renewed the canons enacted at the previous
synods of 1567 and 1575.
[57] Since 1557, the ordaining bishop had been the bishop of Cochin.
The Portuguese founded Latin seminaries for the Syro-Malabarese, thus
effecting a gradual introduction of Latin canon law—Cranganore under
the Franciscans, Carturte under the Dominicans, and Vaipicota (1585)
under the Jesuits.

eighth agreed to appoint an able assistant bishop, [58] as Mar
Abraham was old and infirm, and at the same time unac-
quainted with Latin rites and ceremonies.

The tenth and last canon affecting the native church
forbade the reception of a bishop in Malabar unless he had
brought letters of commendation from either the pope or
the Chaldean patriarch.

The use of Roman books by the Syrians was contrary
to the wishes of the pope, but the Portuguese had become
obsessed with the idea that what was different from the
Latin rite must be in some way heretical. Up to the time
of this synod, the suggestions made by the Jesuits and others
in respect to alterations in the liturgy and ceremonial of the
Malabarese had been well received, and we find that Mar
Joseph [59] had not only introduced Roman vestments and
azyme bread, but he had also taught himself to say Mass in
Latin, in order to please the Portuguese. Now, however,
a very real change in their attitude became apparent, and
Latin interference was resented as leading to the gradual
disappearance of the distinctive Malabarese rites and
customs.

Mar Abraham was again delated to Rome, and Clement VIII (1592-1605) sent a rescript to the archbishop of
Goa in respect to the good faith of the bishop. The pope
directed that he should be summoned to Goa, where he
might answer once and for all the charges that had been
brought against him. The order, however, was unheeded
by the Portuguese, who throughout the whole affair seemed
incapable of honest dealing. In 1595, Mar Abraham became
very ill, but he lived for another two years (1597) before

[58] A Jesuit assistant bishop was appointed.
[59] *De Fontibus Juris Ecclesiastici Syro-Malankarensium, serie II,*
fascic. VIII, p. 44.

he was summoned to a Judge concerning whose impartiality there could be no doubt.

The death of the last of the old Syro-Malabarese hierarchy was announced by the viceroy in a letter (February 6, 1597) to the archbishop of Goa, who was on a visitation at Damao, but even after his decease the memory of Mar Abraham was attacked, and the Portuguese insinuated that he had refused the sacraments on his death-bed.

The Malabarese made repeated attempts to obtain another native bishop, but the Latin authorities [60] determined that so long as they were in India there would never be another Syrian in the episcopate. Alexius de Menezes, archbishop of Goa, writing on December 19,1597, to the Latin titular patriarch of Jerusalem, who resided in Rome, showed how his avowed object was to destroy the old Eastern church: "The priests with many of the people held a meeting and took an oath that in case his holiness appointed a Syrian bishop, they would obey him, but if he sends a Latin bishop, they will consider what course they will adopt. I propose to purify all the churches from the heresy and errors which they hold, giving them the pure doctrine of the Catholic faith, taking from them all the heretical books that they possess... I humbly suggest that he (the new Latin bishop, preferably a Jesuit) be instructed to extinguish

[60] The precautions which were taken to prevent a bishop from "Babylon" coming into the country have been well described by Raulin: "Ne autem caveretur, successoris Chaldei accessus, qui timebatur, ad Ormuzium unicam viam exploratores missi sunt, qui caverent, ne aliquis ecclesiasticorum e Chaldea, Perside, aut Armeni (Aramaea) transiret in Indiam absque speciali Goensi facultate In omnibus propterea portubus Indiae inquisitum fuit in exteros quoscumque illuc adventantes, ac diligenter cautum, ne personati aut nautae, aut trapezitae (quod erat frequens) larvis, episcopi vel presbyteri Babylonici aditum ad eam regionem invenirent..."

29 - A. A. KING, The Rites of Eastern Christendom - 2nd Vol.

little by little the Syrian language, which is not natural. His priests should learn the Latin language, because the Syriac language is the channel through which all that heresy flows. A good administrator ought to replace Syriac by Latin. What is most important of all is that the bishop be a suffragan of this city, as is at present the bishop of Cochin, his near neighbour."

It would seem that the last sentence of the letter gives the real clue to the attitude of the authorities at Goa, but many of the statements, expressed or inferred, have little foundation in fact. The archbishop condemned the patriarch of Babylon as a "public Nestorian heretic," notwithstanding the fact that he, Simon Denha, in 1580 had sent a profession of faith to Rome, and had been confirmed by the pope in his office. Permission for the archdeacon of Mar Abraham to be consecrated bishop of Palur was granted at the request of this same "Nestorian heretic," and there is no evidence that Simon Denha ever wavered in his loyalty to the Apostolic See. In fact, the synod held at Goa in 1585 bore witness to his orthodoxy, but the position had so far worsened that Menezes saw Nestorianism in everything that was not expressly Latin. The archbishop, in the circular convening the synod of 1599, declared that he is "determined and prepared to go in person to take possession of the bishopric" of the Syrians. A rather high-handed procedure, when he had received no confirmatory mandate from the pope. Then, with a strange admixture of inconsistency, Menezes continues: "We were also moved by the piety of the people and the mercy God had shewn them in having preserved so many thousand souls in the faith of our Lord Jesus Christ, from the time that the holy Apostle Thomas preached unto them until this day... By virtue of holy obedience, also, and upon pain of excommunication," the archdeacon of this diocese and all the priests were to come to this synod, together with four representatives from every town and village. Surely, avowed Nestorians would not be praised for their "piety" by a man of the mentality of Menezes, nor could they be summoned to a Catholic council "by virtue of holy obedience;" while threats of excommunication mean little to those who are already outside the Church.

The synod of Diamper, held on June 20-26, 1599, was intended to sound the death knell of the Syrian church of Malabar. No native bishop was present to defend the usages of his church, and the procedings were not only one-sided, but expressed many things contrary to the truth. Giamil, [61] with his facts taken from the Vatican archives, has shown conclusively that what was effected by the Portuguese in regard to the native church of Malabar was done in open disobedience to the wishes and commands of the pope. The fourth decree of the first session of the synod admonishes and orders all Christians, not only ecclesiastics, to confess their sins. All priests were to say Mass and the others to receive the sacrament of the altar for the success of the synod, for which intent there were to be every day two solemn masses, one of the Latins to the Holy Spirit and

---

[61] "*Item perperam Syro-Chaldaicis Malabaribus nonnullos tribuunt errores, quos revera non habent, vel qui errores non sunt, sed peculiares quidam Ecclesiae Syro-Orientalis Ritus in Sacramentorum praesertim administratione usurpati ut scite animadvertit etiam doctissimus Assemanus* (in Bibl. O. 7. 3, pars 2, p. 391) ... *quia multa, ibi facta fuerunt vi per auctoritatem civilem ... et multa contra antiqua et perpetua decreta Sedis Apostolicae, ne quid innovetur aut immutetur in Ritibus Orientalibus, nisi quod contra fidem et mores forte ... Aliqua etiam contra sanam doctrinam ... Menesem, Goveam et Patres Diamperenses in synodi illius decretis peccasse et errasse tum facto tum jure, contra praxim Sanctae Ecclesiae et mentem Summorum RR. Pontificum circa tutelam et integritatem Rituum Orientalium.*" *Genuinae Relationes inter Sedem Apostolicam et Chaldaeorum Ecclesiam*, p. 610, Rome, 1902.

the other of the Syrians in honour of our Lady. It is note-
worthy that these injunctions were issued on the first day
of the synod, whereas on the third day the Syriac service
books were discussed, and certain passages were condemned
as "impious, sacrilegious and a spontaneous outcome of the
Nestorian heresy."   In spite, however, of the wish of the
archbishop to have the Eastern liturgy finally superseded
by that of the Roman Church, the synod of Diamper confined itself to certain verbal changes made with a view to
purge the text of real or supposed Nestorianism, and no
decree whatsoever was issued affecting the relative order of
the different parts of the Mass. This we shall see in detail
later on in the chapter. "The synod," by the fifteenth
decree, "commands in virtue of holy obedience and under
pain of excommunication the priests and deacons and others
whosoever of whatever dignity or rank in this bishopric to
hand over to the most illustrious metropolitan, in person or
through deputies, all books whatsoever written in Syriac,
within two months after the publication of this decree has
come to their knowledge. Under the same precept of obedience and excommunication no one in this bishopric, of
whatever rank he may be, shall dare to copy any books in
Syriac unless the prelate has given him permission in writing
to do it, the book to copy, for which permission is granted,
being expressly mentioned."   It has been said that as a
result of this decree there was a wholesale destruction of
books, on the same lines as that carried out by the Spaniards
after their capture of Seville from the Arabs (1248), but
in actual fact there is no evidence of any such holocaust.
It would seem probable that Dom Alexius originally intended to do this, as the synod [62] spoke of purging these

---

[62] Thus, the first of the decrees on the subject: "*Qua de causa libri
omnes Sacrificii Rituales, sive Missales, quippe qui fuerunt ab haereticis*

books of certain errors and of cutting, tearing up and burning the offices specially consecrated to these heretics. The lack of books, however, restrained the archbishop from a general literary *auto da fé*, and he confined himself to a visitation of the native churches, accompanied by "learned men skilled in the Chaldean language," who brought with them a list of those alterations which the synod had considered to be of paramount importance. Even Diamper, [63] however, had envisaged the permissive use of the ancient rites: "*utque antiquus ritus, quantum patitur fidei sinceritas, ac doctrinae puritas, servetur.*" Breviaries [64] and other books received a similar reprieve owing to the impossibility of replacing them, and they were merely altered in those passages which might be patient of a Nestorian interpretation. The fourth decree of the eighth session of the synod ordered the Roman mass to be translated into Syriac: "Forasmuch as the Syrian mass is too long for priests that have a mind to celebrate daily, the synod doth grant licence for the translating of the Roman mass into Syriac, desiring the Rev. Fr. Roz, S. J. to undertake the work... The synod

---

nestorianis depravati in ignem projici deberent. Verum cum aliorum copia desit quibus celebrari possit quamdiu dominus noster papa, quid agere oporteat non decreverit, aut missalia chaldaice conscripta prout instanter, ac humillime synodus supplicat non miserit: praecepit synodus illa expurgari, et quae sequuntur interferri; ceterum ante expurgationem quam illius metropolitanus (Menezes) in visitatione simul cum doctis viris et chaldaicae linguae peritis quos ad id deputaverit perficiet, sacerdotum nullus iis utatur." Raulin. *Hist. Eccles. Mal.*, p. 145, ap. *Dict. d'Archéol. Chrét. et de Lit.*, t. X, col. 1276.

[63] *Dict. d'Archéol. Chrét. et de Lit. Ibid.*

[64] "*Quos libros omnes, et breviaria, licet digna sint quae igni tradantur... attamen synodus emendari praecipit, eo quod in hac dioecesi alii sacri libri non suppetant, quibus sacerdotes utantur in celebrandis divinis officiis.*" Actio III, decret. 15. RAULIN, *Hist. Eccles. Mal.*, pp. 106-7; ap. *Dict. d'Archéol. Chrét. et de Lit.* IX, col. 1276.

desires that the bishops of these parts give licence that the priests of this diocese, having letters dimissory from their prelates, that do not know how to say mass in Latin, may be permitted to say the Syrian mass in their churches or at least the Romam translated with all its ceremonies into Syriac."

The synod also prohibited some Brahmin customs which had been retained, such as the wearing of a tuft of hair in the centre of the head, the boring of the ears for the wearing of earrings, and the compulsory taking of a bath if a *nair* (a member of a lower caste) had been touched.

The high-handed action of the Portuguese at Diamper, carried out without the knowledge or approval of Rome, has been described as "a change which not even the Holy See in the plenitude of its authority has effected anywhere in the world: history [65] does not record such sweeping changes in the rites, ceremonies and customs of a church in any other part of the world."

The Maronite Assemani, who wrote in Rome under the very eyes of Pope Innocent XI (1676-1689), said that the *acta* of the synod were "mostly the outcome of misguided zeal, ignorance of the Syriac rite and language, and of the ancient Eastern rites, together with an excessive study of Roman ceremonials."

In one respect, however, writers in the past have exaggerated the work of the synod of Diamper, in asserting that the eucharistic liturgy of the church of Malabar was seriously mutilated as a result of the enactments of the council.

---

[65] The synod, in the person of the archbishop of Goa, anathematised Simon Denha, the Chaldean patriarch, despite the fact that he had received the pallium from the pope: "*nulloque expectato consensu, aut nominatione a Patriarcha Babylonico, quem reiicio, damno et anathematizo tamquam hereticum Nestorianum schismaticum et extra obedientiam Sanctae Romanae Ecclesiae et idcirco extra aeternam salutem!*"

This is not the case, and only the following alterations[66] were ordered:

a) The formula of institution and consecration was to be that of the Roman church. *b*) There was to be an elevation and genuflection after each consecration. *c*) The Nicene creed must follow the Roman text. *d*) Words in some of the prayers were inserted, taken away or altered. *e*) The formula: "Behold the living and life-giving bread" was to be said after the *second* consecration and elevation. *f*) The rite of intinction, in which the precious blood soaked the sacred bread, was abolished.

Thus, it can be readily seen that the Mass[67] of Menezes, with the exception of the comparatively few alterations noted above, was identical with the liturgy which the Malabarese were accustomed to celebrate, and any other divergence from the Chaldean rite had been effected earlier in the century.

The archbishop himself made a profession of faith at the synod, and required the Syrian representatives to do the same, but the Christians and *cathanars* (priests) murmured, saying: "they were Christians and they had faith; how then could they profess the faith, showing that they had not had it before". The metropolitan answered that it was a duty, which he himself had performed, and they were not to grumble at the possibly implied doubt, lest it might be taken to mean that they had not the same faith before. They were only asked to imitate him, and "the duty of every Christian was to profess his faith when he is required to

---

[66] HANSSENS, *Instit. Liturg. de Rit. Orient.*, T. II, part. I, p. 502.

[67] The Syro-Malabar Mass, as revised by the authority of the synod of Diamper, has been published by Gouvea (1606), Le Brun (1726), Raulin (1745), and others.

do so or when he is suspected to doubt about any part of the faith."

George, the archdeacon, was now the head of the church of Malabar, and, although he was the nominee of the Chaldean patriarch and *persona grata* with the pope, he was required to make a very special profession of faith: "... I do also promise, vow and swear to God on this cross and these holy gospels, never to receive into this church and bishopric of the Serra, any bishop, archbishop, prelate, pastor or governor whatsoever, but what shall be immediately appointed by the holy Apostolical See and the bishop of Rome, and that whomsoever he shall appoint, I will receive and obey as my true pastor, *without expecting any message from or having any further dependence upon the Patriarch of Babylon.*"

Under the influence of the Portuguese, a succession of Jesuit bishops was appointed to rule the Syrian church of Malabar. Francis Foz in 1601 was consecrated bishop of Angamaly at Goa, but four years later (1605) he was translated to the newly erected archbishopric of Cranganore. He died on February 18,1624, at his residence in Parur. Search was made for his tombstone in 1888 at the first visitation of the vicar apostolic of Trichur, and, when found, it was affixed to the inner wall of the church.

Stephen de Brito, the second Jesuit bishop, died on December 2,1641, and was succeeded by Francis Garcia, who since 1637 had been coadjutor with right of succession. The choice was not a happy one, and the bishop has been described as obstinate, sarcastic and devoid of tact. These Jesuit bishops sometimes appointed members of their society to be rectors of Syrian parishes, and in 1608 Archdeacon George protested against this injustice to the nuncio at Lisbon. No answer was forthcoming, but a second letter

(1628) was forwarded to Rome (1630), with the admission of the nuncio that the alleged grievances were substantially true. In 1632, the intrepid archdeacon († 1637), together with the Syrian Clergy and representatives of the laity, sent from Edapally [68] a petition to the king of Portugal, praising the work done by Mar Abraham, and complaining of the errors and confusion that was caused by the new bishop's ignorance of the Syriac language.

When Thomas de Campo was archdeacon, as it seemed impossible to obtain any redress from the Portuguese for the intolerable state of affairs, a deputation was sent to ask the Chaldean patriarch to send a bishop to Malabar. Ahatalla [69] arrived in India in 1652, and gave to two deacons, who were on pilgrimage at Mylapore, a letter for the Malabarese clergy, in which he styled himself "Patriarch of India and China." The Portuguese, although the bishop claimed full authority from the pope, seized him and sent him, by way of Cochin, to Goa. A number of Malabarese appeared before the fort at Cochin, demanding his release, but they must have thought this unlikely, as they said that if the Jesuits had killed him "let any other person of the four religious orders come here, by order of the supreme pontiff, a man who knows Syriac and can teach us and help us in our offices, except the Fathers of St. Paul [70] whom we do not at all desire, because they are enemies of us and of the holy Mother Church at Rome; with that exception let anybody come and we are ready to obey without hesitation."

No reply was given to this pitiful request, and a rumour was circulated that Ahatalla had been drowned at Cochin

[68] Portuguese, Rapolin.
[69] Jaballa, Deusdedit.
[70] Members of the Society of Jesus, so called because they were first sent to Malabar from St. Paul's College, Goa.

by the Portuguese.   The loyalty of the people was now
strained to breaking point, and action was determined upon.
On January 3,1654, an assembly was held in the church at
Mattancherry, when all, holding a rope which was tied to
a monument called the Cunan Cross, took an oath that they
would no longer be subject to the Jesuits.   Mar Elias, about
seventy-three years earlier, had prophesied to the pope that
the rule of Portugal would prove disastrous to the church
of Malabar. A council at Alengad on May 22 of the same
year enjoined the "consecration" of the archdeacon as
bishop by the laying on of the hands of twelve priests.   Four
councillors or consultors were appointed to assist him, of
whom one, Ittythoman Angilimootil of Kallucherry, from
his prominence in furthering the schism, was known as the
"hero of the Syrians."   This "hero" was responsible for the
forged letter, purporting to come from the pope, in which
the priests were empowered to "consecrate" the archdeacon.
It is thus clearly evident that the quarrel was with the Portuguese, especially with those who were Jesuits, and in no
way hostile to Rome.   Indeed, a manifesto explicitly stated
this: "Therefore, since our people who went to San Thomé
and met the said patriarch received a letter and a patent
from him, which they brought to us, by which we are governed, and since we have made an archbishop by the order
and command of the patriarch, who came *by the mandate
of the supreme pontiff and of the holy mother Church of
Rome* we shall live with the said archbishop... Because no
one listened to the complaints that the Malabarese made at
Cochin, therefore we here assembled ordain that since they
have *paid no attention to the mandate of the supreme pontiff
and of the holy mother Church of Rome* and of our prelate,
and as the Fathers of St. Paul are enemies to us and of the
holy mother Church of Rome (*sic*), we shall never hold

friendship with them until we see the patriarch with our own eyes, and we shall pay no attention to the archbishop of that order."

The Malabarese, however, were too good theologians not to have doubts about the validity of the proceedings, and not long after the schism two of the councillors, Alexander Kadavil and Alexander Palliveetil (de Campo), having gained the support of twenty-five churches, went to Cranganore and made their submission to the Jesuit archbishop.   In 1655, Alexander Paliveetil, in a meeting at Edapally, agreed to invite the Carmelites of Goa to Malabar, and, through them, letters were sent to the prior of the Scala convent in Rome and to the pope. Alexander VII (1655-1667) welcomed the proposal and sent three fathers to the country, who, arriving in February 1657, had by the following year reconciled no less than forty-four churches. It was reckoned [71] that one hundred and fifty thousand in the diocese of Angamaly had gone into schism.   The papal commissary, Fr. Joseph Sebastiani, especially commended the assistance of Alexander Kadavil in the work of reconciliation: "the most learned and the most popular of the priests of Malabar This priest, who had once consented to the consecration of the pseudo-bishop, which was the cause of the introduction of schism in Malabar, was travelling with me everywhere preaching zealously against the schism."   The commissary returned to Rome, and in 1661 came back to Malabar as bishop of Hierapolis and apostolic administrator, with permission to consecrate one or two Malabarese as vicars apostolic, so that the church might be freed from the jurisdiction of the Portuguese Jesuits.

[71] From a letter (January 26, 1656) which the pope had given to his commissary, Fr. Joseph Sebastiani.

The Coming of the Dutch

Another factor, however, had appeared in south India, the Protestant Dutch, who succeded in January 1663 in capturing Cochin. The change of rule necessitated the withdrawal of the Italian Carmelites, and Alexander de Campo was consecrated titular bishop of Megara, and governed the church of Malabar for twenty-five years. Eighty-four churches, in the two years preceding his elevation to the episcopate, are said to have been reconciled, leaving thirty-two to the schismatic archdeacon (Thomas). In 1673, the Carmelites came to Verapoly, which has remained their headquarters to the present day. Van Rheede, the Dutch governor, in the following year gave permission for Rome to be petitioned to sanction a coadjutor bishop. Four Carmelites were chosen to proceed with the election, and, since the pope wished for a native episcopate, Bishop Alexander put forward the name of Fr. Mathew. The choice, however, was set aside and Raphael Figueredo, an East Indian Portuguese of the Latin rite, was appointed (1667). Bishop Alexander de Campo [72] died on December 23, 1687, and his picture still hangs in the church of Kuravalangad, where he is buried. The Malabarese had an especial veneration for the family, which claimed that St. Thomas had ordained some of its members as priests.

The refusal of the Carmelites to elect a native bishop effectively prevented the reconciliation of the remaining schismatics, and the new Latin auxiliary excommunicated the vicar general of Bishop Alexander, Fr. George, who was parish priest of Mattancherry. The Carmelites, who now

[72] De Campo is the Portuguese for the Indian family name Pakalomattam, which means literally *campus solis*.

recognised their mistake, appealed to the pope, who on February 6, 1687, ordered Custodius de Pinho, vicar apostolic of the great mogul, to look into the matter. As a result of the enquiry, Rome deposed Figueredo (January 16,1694) and appointed Custodius, who died before he was able to take charge of the vicariate. In 1700, the Carmelite Angelus Francis became vicar general of Malabar, and received consecration in the following year from the Chaldean bishop Mar Simon at Alengad. Garcia was succeded in the archbishopric of Cranganore by another Jesuit, Ribeiro (1701-1716), and members of the Society of Jesus continued to hold the see until 1771. The coming of the Dutch, however, had curtailed the extent of the diocese, which now only comprised the territory of the Zamorin of Calicut, where Holland had no control. Over the remaining part of the country, the Carmelites continued their spiritual supervision for two hundred years, during which time disputes were infrequent, although several parishes were latinised. The Malabarese, however, still petitioned Rome that they might be allowed to have their own bishops. From time to time Chaldean prelates came to the country to study the situation on the spot, but, as they were unpopular with the Carmelites, they were soon compelled to leave India. Thus, Mar Simon visited Malabar in 1701 and Mar Gabriel in 1708. The latter was expressly forbidden by Rome to interfere in the affairs of the Indian church. In 1773, a serious dispute, which lasted a considerable time, arose at the funeral of Bishop Florentius, when the points at issue concerned the participation of the Syrian clergy and the rite to be used in the obsequies.

The dissidents in the meanwhile continued to be governed by archdeacons, who had taken the title of "bishops." In 1700, a joint petition was sent to the Catholic Chaldean patriarch applying for the reception of valid orders, but Mar Simon, who had the necessary faculties, was removed from the country before the hierarchy could be established. Four years later (1704), a request was made that Archdeacon Thomas IV might be raised to the episcopate, with the assurance that the only motive for the schism had been interference from the Paulists (Jesuits).

In spite of another disappointment, reconciliation was sought for a third time in 1778, when Thomas VI (Dionysius I), who six years earlier (1772) had received consecration at Viranam from Mar Gregorius, a Jacobite bishop, requested to be admitted to communion with the Apostolic See, together with his flock. The Latin bishops, whether rightly or not, doubted his sincerity, and opposed his recognition by Rome. Nothing daunted, Thomas sought the help of Joseph Cariatta, a Malabarese priest and *alumnus* of the Propaganda College, who obtaining the necessary faculties, received consecration in 1783 at Lisbon as archbishop of Cranganore. Again, however, a mysterious death frustrated the hopes of the Malabarese, and, before the reconciliation of the dissidents could be effected, Archbishop Cariatta had died at Goa. Fr. Parayammakal, his secretary and companion, whom he had already appointed administrator of the archdiocese, was confirmed in his office by the Latin metropolitan of Goa, and until 1799 governed the Catholics of the Eastern rite. Fr. Parayammakal and Matthew Thatchil Tharakan, a leading layman, worked hard for the return of the schismatics, but Latin opposition proved too strong, and Joseph Soledad, the Portuguese Carmelite bishop of Cochin, refused to recognise the episcopal status of the Jacobite bishop. The historian Paulinus, [73] a member

[73] *India Orientalis*, p. 124.

of the same Order, called the Latin prelate: *"Vir asperi ingenii et nemini indulgens, infinitos in ora Travancordis excitavit tumultus."* The last golden opportunity for healing the schism had been lost, and not long afterwards the dissidents came under the disintegrating influence of Protestantism. As we have seen, christological questions did not greatly interest the Malabarese, and by accepting in 1655 Gregory, the West Syrian metropolitan of Jerusalem, the schismatics, who were known as the *Puthenkoottukar* or "New Party," came to be called "Jacobites," although it was not until 1772 that orders were obtained from that source. Catholics were the *Pazhekuttukar* or "Old Party."

It would seem that the East Syrian liturgy was not finally abandoned by the dissidents until some time after 1846.

The Coming of the English.
Modern History of the Church of Malabar

The second Mysore War (1790-1792) left England in undisputed supremacy in south India, and in 1795 the rajahs of Cochin and Travancore became vassals of Great Britain. This conquest introduced a new religious factor into Malabar, the Church of England.

The Church Missionary Society arrived in 1816, and some years later set itself in opposition to the Jacobite metropolitan, who retaliated by excommunicating those of his subjects who changed their beliefs in a Protestant direction. The result of the new teaching was to cause an even greater disintegration of Malabar Christianity than the general tactlessness of the Catholic Portuguese. In 1835, a Protestantized body came into existence, whose members arrogated to themselves the title of "St. Thomas Christians."

A further division in the dissident church resulted in 1909 from a visit of the Jacobite patriarch of Antioch, and a party was formed in opposition to his claim to regulate the temporal affairs of the church.

In 1801, the Catholic Malabarese obtained a native administrator of Cranganore in the person of Dr. George Shankurikel, an alumnus of the Propaganda College, Rome, but his successor was Portuguese.

By the brief *Multa praeclare* (April 24, 1838), Pope Gregory XVI temporarily abolished the Padroado [74] jurisdiction, together with the dioceses of Cranganore, Cochin and Mylapore; while the jurisdiction of the archbishop of Goa was restricted to actual Portuguese territory. The Carmelite vicar apostolic of Verapoly received the honorific title of "archbishop of Cranganore."

In 1886, the bull *Humanae salutis auctor* restored the sees of Cochin and Mylapore, and at the same time straightened out the *Padroado* dispute.

Indian Carmelite tertiaries were started in 1831 at Mannanam, and they were affiliated in 1860 to the discalced order.

The people, however, after three centuries of waiting still cried out for a native bishop of their own rite, even going to the length of forming a fresh schism in order to attain their end.

In 1858, Antony Thondanatta went to Mosul, where he prevailed upon Mar Thomas Roccos to go to Malabar (1861). The prelate obtained some local support, but within a year he was compelled by Pope Pius IX to return to Mesopo-

[74] Portuguese, "patronage." An ancient privilege of the crown of Portugal of naming bishops for vacant sees in territory where Portuguese subjects were settled. The "double jurisdiction" of Portugal and Propaganda was finally abolished in 1928.

tamia. The instigator of the movement in 1863 submitted
to the Church, and discipline was restored, but some years
later he again went to Mosul, where he received episcopal
consecration in the name of Ebed Jesu, at the hands of
the Nestorian patriarch, since this had been refused him by
the Chaldean Mar Audo. Once again Antony Thondanatta was reconciled, but a further crisis was caused by the
arrival in Malabar of Mar Elias Mellus, Chaldean bishop
of Akra (1874), who, in spite of the prohibition by Rome,
was encouraged by Mar Audo to reorganise the sect. The
intruding bishop was recalled in 1877 by Mar Audo when
he was threatened with excommunication, but for the third
and last time Antony Thondanatta left the Catholic Church
and put himself at the head of the schismatics, whom he
ruled until his death in 1900. Then for eight years the sect
was without a head, until in 1908 the Anglican Church
obtained a bishop for them in Mar Abimilech Timothy,
archdeacon of the Nestorian patriarchal court at Kotchanes,
who was consecrated by his patriarch with the title of
"Metropolitan of Malabar and of the Indies." The new
bishop,[75] who came arrayed in Latin vestments, including
an immense Roman mitre and a crozier, attempted to pro-
testantise his flock,[76] but he was met with a fierce opposition
from those who, Nestorian but in name, retained most or
all of the Catholic dogmas.

The majority of the Malabarese, in spite of the failure
of all their efforts to obtain a redress of their legitimate
grievances, remained faithful to Rome, and in 1887 a first

[75] HEAZELL-MARGOLIOUTH, *Kurds and Christians*, p. 196. London,
1913.
[76] About 1500 in number, living in Trichur. There is some doubt
as to whether the Mellusians have retained the "romanised" rite or
returned to that of the Nestorians.

20 - A. A. KING, *The Rites of Eastern Christendom* - 2nd Vol.

step was made towards the fulfilment of their hopes. In that year, Pope Leo XIII (1878-1903), by the brief *Quod jam-pridem,* transferred the government of the Malabar Syrian Church from Verapoly and the *Padroado* administrator at Cranganore to two Latin vicars apostolic at Trichur and Kottayam respectively. Kottayam, however, was not a Catholic centre, and in May 1891 the place of residence was was removed to Changanacherry, where the St. John Berchman's High School, the first of its kind in Malabar, was founded. The second stage in the restoration of the hierarchy was reached on July 28, 1896, when, by the brief *Quae rei sacrae,* three *native* vicars apostolic were appointed, —for Trichur, Ernakulam, Changanacherry. The last named prelate was a Suddist [77] and therefore distasteful to the Nordist majority, [78] who on October 15, 1896, petitioned the pope against him. The probable origin of these two castes has been already shewn, and such native leaders as the Portuguese permitted the church of Malabar to have were all Nordists. [79] A climax was reached on August 28, 1911, when the Nordists obtained a vicar apostolic of their own at Changanacherry. The following day, however, the brief *In universi Christiani* established a *"novum Vicariatum"* at Kottayam *"pro gente Sudistica."* A Belgian Jesuit, once a missionary in India, writing in the *Catholic Herald of India* [80] in reference to the brief *Quae rei sacrae,* said: "For three centuries the European missionaries went on footling and blundering and worrying the poor Syrians with their Latin bishops, until Leo XIII got enough of it and, in face

[77] Still termed *Antchipallikars,* " those who have only five churches."
[78] More than sixteen times greater than the Suddists.
[79] All the Jacobite bishops until 1910 had been Nordists.
[80] January 30, 1924.

of a strong opposition, appointed three Indian Syrian bishops."

At long last, the legitimate claims of the Malabarese were fully conceded, and Pope Pius XI (1922-1939) in a consistory [81] held on December 20, 1923, declared his intention of creating for the Syro-Malabar rite a province (Ernakulam) with three suffragan sees (Trichur, Changa-nacherry, Kottayam), dependent, through the apostolic del-egate to the East Indies, on the Sacred Congregation for the Eastern Church.

Seminaries and Religious Orders

Priests, who are known as *cathanars* ("Lord's men"), are educated at Puttenpally [82] (Travancore, directed by the Belgian Jesuits, 1866); St. Joseph's Mangalore; Propaganda College, Rome; and the Pontifical Seminary at Kandy (Ceylon, directed by the Jesuits, 1893).

As a point of interest, we may note that until recent

[81] "*Eodemque Sacro Consilio Nobis operam narrante, efficimus, Dei munere ut ex Vicariatibus Apostolicis Syro-Malabaricis quattuor Sedes Episcopales totidem institueremus, quarum metropolis Ernakulam: Quod quidem ideo libentissime hic commemoramus, quia non parum videmur afferre laetitiae dilectissimis filiis catholicis eas regiones inco-lentibus; quibus maxime fausta jam adest, sancti Thomae Apostoli na-talis dies. Id autem omnino postulabat et egregia apud eos rei catholicae temperatio; et praeclari quos ii Vicariatus habuerant sub indigenis pro-prii ritus Episcopis in religione progressus; et eorum fidelium vere con-sentanei christianae professioni mores; et singularis eorumdem erga Bea-tissimam Virginem Mariam pietas atque in Clerum, in Episcopos praeci-pueque in hanc Apostolicam Sedem summa observantia.*"

[82] In 1866, the seminary was moved from Verapoly, where the Car-melites had established a college in 1675 for all the clergy of Malabar. Since the restoration of the hierarchy, every diocese has its own minor seminary; Trichur has also a major college; while for the other sees there is an interritual seminary at Alwaye (Travancore).

times the candidates for the first minor order were required
to present letters in which the consent of the parishoners
was expressed.

Carmelite tertiaries of the Malabarese rite (*Karmilitha
Nishpatkuka Munnam Sabha*) were founded in 1831 by
Thomas Palakal and Thomas Porukara at Mannanam. In
1854 they were canonically approved, and in 1906 received
their present rule of life. Pope Pius IX in 1861 sent a letter
of commendation to the tertiaries, in which he praised their
work in combatting the schismatic movements of Roccos and
Mellus. The residence of the prior general is at Thevara
near Ernakulam. According to the most recent statistics,
there are 27 houses of the Congregation, with a total of 225
priests, 70 lay brothers and 132 students (professed and
novices).

A corresponding order for women was started in 1867,
which, twenty years later, received a separate organisation
for the oriental rite.

In addition, there are at least four other congregations
for women.

A foundation of Oblates of the Sacred Heart for men
religious of the Oriental rite has been established in recent
years in the diocese of Kottayam, and in 1925 an Eastern
branch of the Lazarists was formed.

It was computed that the regular clergy in 1912 num-
bered 72 and the sisters 347; while the official statistics for
1031 showed 532, 531 faithful of the rite, with 636 secular
priests, all strictly bound to celibacy, and 297 religious with
16 houses. By 1946, the numbers had greatly increased,
and the faithful were estimated to be 848, 521, with a
corresponding increase of priests, secular and religious.

Monuments

Monumental evidence of Christianity, dating from the 9th century, is found in four granite crosses with Pahlevi inscriptions.

Those at Mount St. Thomas (Mylapore) and Kottayam bear the words: [83] "The punishment by the Cross was of suffering of him, who is the true Christ, God above and Guide ever pure."

The Mylapore cross [84] has an additional inscription: "My Lord Christ, have mercy upon Afras, son of Chaharbukht the Syrian, who cut this." Who is this Afras? Is it possible that he was the companion of Mar Sapor who in the 9th century came to Quilon? Other crosses were erected in the country between the years 1547 and 1599.

The churches of the Malabar Jacobites, almost *hallen kirchen* [85] in appearance, have a profusion of surface ornament, which gives them a strangely Hindu aspect. Prior to the coming of the Portuguese, the churches resembled pagodas. The buildings of the Catholics are similar to those of the dissidents, but their interior arrangements have been latinised.

Liturgical Language

The language of the liturgy is Syriac, the Chaldean form in the Catholic Malabarese rite and the West Syrian in the Jacobite and Malankara rites.

---

[83] Cf. Chinese Stone.

[84] *Journal of Theological Studies.* C. P. T. Winkworth. April, 1929.

[85] A name given to those brick churches of hall-like appearance, erected in the 14th and 15th centuries in north Germany and Holland.

Calendar

The calendar [86] is almost entirely Roman, although a few eastern commemorations have been retained. There are thirteen days of obligation—five of our Lord, five of our Lady, All Saints, St. Thomas [87] (July 3) and St. Peter and St. Paul.

Especial devotion is shown to the passion, the sorrows of our Lady, St. Joseph, St. George and St. Sebastian.

St. George is greatly venerated by the Indians, without distinction of caste or creed, and all call him *valyachan*, "grandpapa."

The Advent abstinence begins on December 1, and the fast of Lent on the Monday *preceding* Ash Wednesday; while, in addition to Fridays, the Ember days, vigils, Saturdays and the days of the fast of Nineveh [88] are observed. The synod of Diamper [89] ordered the last named fast to be strictly kept. A fast [90] of eight days before the Nativity of our Lady (September 8), only binding on virgins and peculiar to Malabar, was obligatory until recent times. To-day many keep the fast from a motive of piety.

---

[86] Francis Dionysius, writing from Cochin to Rome in 1578, said: "The St. Thomas Christians have some of our feasts as those of our Lord and the Assumption. Of late some feasts of ours have been introduced amongst them..." Jesuit Archives, Goa, 12, 439: original.

[87] The West Syrian calendar has two feasts of St. Thomas - October 6 (martyrdom) and July 3 (translation). The synod of Diamper (VIII, 9; cf. *de sacr.*, 12) admitted December 18 as a feast, the day on which the cross of St. Thomas was accustomed to sweat.

[88] The fast begins on the 18th day before the Ist day of Lent. It is known as *Munna-norba* (*munna*, "three" (days); *nojerba*, "fast").

[89] *Act. VIII, decret.* 10.

[90] Synod of Diamper, *Act.*, VIII, *decret.* 10; *De Fontibus Juris Ecclesiastici Syro-Malankarensium.* Serie II, fascicolo VIII.

Many Western devotions and practices have been adopted, such as Benediction, rosary, stations of the cross, and the wearing of the Carmelite scapular.

Vestments

The Malabarese use Roman vestments. [91]   Gouvea [92] writes of "an archbishop" sent from "Babylon," who introduced "our vestments in the Roman manner" and "commanded the use of our wine and of our hosts." This "archbishop" seems to have been Joseph, brother of John Sulaka the Catholic patriarch (1552-1555), who was sent by his successor, Ebed Jesu (1562 onwards).

Eucharistic Bread and Wine

It would seem that leavened bread was used in the liturgy until the end of the 16th century, and Gouvea [93] writes of a strange practice that existed among the Malabarese. Theophylactus, writing about the year 1090, mentions "*tous Indous*" among those who have fermented bread;

---

[91] The outdoor dress of the clergy is that of the Portuguese in Goa. The white cassock was in use until 1830.

[92] *Jornada do arcebispo de Goa*, pp. 6-7. Coimbra, 1606. It would seem that any assistant at Mass, before the introduction of Roman vestments, was accustomed to wear a stole, even if he was a layman: "*Qui missae ministrabat, etiamsi esset laicus stola diaconorum more super vulgares vestes utebatur, incessanter thurificans et quamplurima cum sacerdote alternis cantans, potiusquam recitans.*" RAULIN, *Historia Ecclesiae Malabaricae*, p. 391.

[93] "The clerics used to sing psalms and hymns of praise—when engaged in making hosts on the tower just above the high altar, and let them down thence to the celebrant at the offertory by means of a string." C. J. Cathanar citing Gouvea in the *Orthodoxy of the St. Thomas Christians*, p. 41, n.

while Josephus Indus, [94] who flourished about 1500, says that the Christians of Malabar use azymes whenever they are able to do so. Assemanus, commenting on Josephus, points out that this does not imply that the Malabarese have given up the use of their traditional eucharistic bread, but only that some of them, to conform to the use of the Latins, have adopted azymes.

At the end of the century, the synod of Diamper seemed to infer the use of fermented bread: "*ne farina cum alia quacumque materia re sit admixta, ut assolet etiam cum pane usuali.*" When, however, in 1712 Gabriel, a Chaldean bishop, came to Malabar, he was forbidden to celebrate Mass until he had signed a profession of faith, in which he promised to use azyme bread exclusively. The Malabarese hosts are a little thicker than those used by the Latins. The synod of Diamper also legislated concerning the preparation of the eucharistic bread: "*Ut in singulis ecclesiis ferreae habeantur formae ad rotundanda atque obsignanda triticea crustula, sive, ut vulgo dicitur, hostias, quae instrumento cito citius unaquaeque ecclesia sibi comparet .... Curabunt insuper vicarii, penes se farinam triticeam perpetuo asservare, e qua hostiae conficiantur .... Nec quibuscumque triticeos orbes conficiendi curam committant, eosque vel per se ipsos, vel per probatae fidei administros, hujusce rei peritos conficiant.*"

The practice of using unfermented wine, commented on by Gouvea and the Chaldean patriarch, Joseph II (1691-1714), is of course unknown among the Catholics.

The altar vessels are of the Latin pattern and shape.

---

[94] Josephi Indi navigatio: "*Consecrant corpus Christi et sanguinem, si tamen id consequi possunt, in azymis, hoc est in pane non fermentato, more nostro.*" Ap. HANSSENS, *Institutiones Liturgicae de Ritibus Orientalibus*, t. II, part I, p. 140.

History of the Rite and Liturgical Books

The Malabarese have the liturgy of the East Syrians, but there is only one anaphora—a version of the Holy Apostles Addai and Mari (*Kudasa dasleeke Kadeese*).

A rite of the Presanctified is now celebrated on Good Friday, but there was no mention of it in the synod of Diamper (1599). An "expurgated" missal [95] was published after the synod, but, as we have seen, the old idea that the liturgy was seriously dislocated at Diamper is substantially false. Gouvea, in a Latin translation attached to the *acta* of the synod, spoke of the rite as "purged of errors and Nestorian blasphemies" by the archbishop of Goa; while Brightman, [96] influenced by the *Jornada*, says: "these texts, which contain the *ordo communis*, the lections (apostles and gospels) and the anaphora of the Apostles, have been purged from real or supposed Nestorianism and considerably dislocated by de Menezes and the synod of Diamper (1599)."

It is true that the text of the liturgy appended to the *acta* of the synod by Gouvea and, later, by Raulin is seen to be seriously dislocated when it is compared with the printed editions of the Nestorian and Chaldean books. This dislocation, however, is now considered to have been due to the sheets of the copy of the missal before the synod having

[95] *Missa qua utebantur antiqui Christiani episcopatus Angamallensis in montanis Malabarici regni apud Indos Orientales, emendata et ab erroribus blasphemiisque Nestorianorum expurgata ab Illustrissimo et Reverendissimo Domino Alexis Menseis Archiepiscopo Goano, Indiae primate in synodo Diocesana Angamallae, Anno 1599 e Syriaco in Latinum Sermonem conversa et exscripta ex Itinerario Lusitanico ejusdem Menesii Coninabricae edito, et ex Bibliotheca Illustrissimi et Reverendissimi Domini Renanti Poterii Bellovacensis Episcopi Franciae Paris deprompto.*

[96] *Op. cit.*, p. LXXVIII.

been bound up in the wrong order. One dislocation, for example, gave the lessons with their prayers after the dismissal of the catechumens: a quite pointless and unliturgical "alteration," and one which Menezes was not the man to make. In any case, he would not deny anything that he might do, and would certainly have given his reasons in the *acta* of the synod. Other dislocations, [97] such as the insertion of the diaconal intercession "And for all the katholikoi" after the epiclesis, are also found in the same place.

In the present missal, however, there are only two deviations from the old order—the placing of the creed after the gospel and the insertion of the consecration immediately before the fraction. The first dislocation is rectified in those solemn Masses which the Malabarese call *râzê*.

Here, the offertory by the priest, as opposed to the prothesis, takes place after the creed, while in the present Nestorian and Chaldean books it occurs after the dismissals, during the anthem of the mysteries.

The ancient expositions of Narsai (*Exposition of the Mysteries*), Abraham Bar Lipheh (*Interpretation of the Offices*) and George of Arbela (*Exposition of the Offices of the Church*) make no mention of it at all, but they give the following order: dismissals, setting of the *oblata* on the altar by the deacons, entrance of the bishop and priests from the nave into the sanctuary, followed immediately by the creed.

[97] Neale and Littledale (*Translations of the Primitive Liturgies*. 7th edition, introduction, pp. XX-XXI) give the old view of throwing all the blame upon Menezes: "it was revised by the Portuguese Archbishop of Goa, Alexis de Menezes and the Synod of Diamper (1599), - a revision which, as even Roman liturgists allow, shows utter ignorance of Oriental Liturgies."

The Nestorian and Chaldean usage thus breaks up the old entrance, which is preserved to-day in the Malabarese *râzâ*.

Diamper was not responsible for the deviation, and the insertion of the words of institution before the fraction was certainly not the work of Dom Alexius Menezes. These words and their historical setting are stated by Gouvea [98] and Raulin, as in the case of the Roman vestments and azyme bread, to have been introduced into the rite by an "archbishop" from "Babylon," and to have been in use for many years prior to the synod. Diamper discussed the actual words of institution and for these the Roman formula was substituted, but the historical setting was *not* imposed by the synod.

Apart from this, and the correction of one reading in the gospel of St. John (V, 28) appearing in the translation, the synod of Diamper ordered thirty-eight changes, [99] but there was no dislocation of the ancient order. The Portuguese by that time were obsessed by the belief that Nestorianism had insinuated itself into such ways of speaking as "Christ," "Jesus" and "Son," so that they thought it necessary to develop them. Thus there was substituted for "Christ," [100] "Jesus Christ his Son our Lord." Six of the changes occur in the second "seal," which is not in the printed books at all.

Of the remainder, the original wording is unchanged in

[98] " *e nesta forma consagravão de muytos annos atègora.*" Jornada.

[99] Of the changes imposed by the synod, 4 occur in formulas reserved to the deacon; 1 in a response made by the faithful; while of those which are in prayers said by the priest - 5 precede the anaphora (*Sursum corda*), 4 are in the anaphora, and 11 in the final blessings. *Dict. d'Archéol. Chrét. et de Lit.*, t. X, part I, col. 1277.

[100] Thus, 15 changes in the wording of the liturgy concerned the title by which the Saviour is named. *Ibid.*

the printed texts; in one, the old wording is retained in some texts, but not in others; in seven, the required alterations have been adopted, though not always in the form prescribed by the synod.

These seven included the addition of clauses which had been omitted from the Nicene creed, so that it might "be such as is sung by the whole Church, and is contained in the Roman missal;" and the substitution of "Mother of God" for "Mother of Christ" (in 2 places); of orthodox saints for heretics (in 2 places); and of the pope for the Nestorian katholikos (in 2 places).

The local edition of the missal published in 1912, which purported to be a "reprint of the 1775 [101] book," substituted the words "katholikos of Romania" for "Eastern katholikos!"

The original text was "may the glorious throne of the Eastern katholikos be blessed," This, in the Latin translation, appeared as *"cathedra gloriosa Romana Catholica,"* and from the Latin the strange English expression, "katholikos of Romania" was evolved.

Yet, for all their dislike of the Syrian church of Malabar, it is clear that the Portuguese archbishop of Goa and the synod of Diamper did not seriously interfere with the eucharistic liturgy. Dom Henri Leclercq [102] has said: *"La liturgie de Malabar n'a pas été "romanisée;" il est possible, à l'aide des actes du synode de Diamper, de la traduction latine de cette liturgie par A. de Gouvea, de l'édition syriaque de 1774 (à Rome) et du texte d'Urmi (Nestorien) de rétablir une part considérable du texte syriaque de la liturgie de Malabar."*

It was, however, otherwise with the Ritual and Pontif-

[101] The missal was published in 1774, not. 1775.
[102] *Dict. d'Archéol. Chrét. et de Lit.,* t. X. H. LECLERCQ, art. *Malabar,* col. 1277.

ical, and the synod of Diamper ordered the Roman books to be translated into Syriac for the use of the Christians of the Syro-Malabar rite.

The commission for the revision of the Eastern liturgical books, which in 1936 was set up in the Congregation for the Oriental Church, has decided to revise the pontifical [103] forthwith. The strange anomaly of ordinations conferred in the Latin of the Roman *pontifical* in a church of the Eastern rite, whose language is Syriac, will therefore be made to cease.

The Congregation, also, has decided to restore the other liturgical books, so that in course of time we may hope to see the Malabarese in full possession of their primitive rite.

About the middle of the 19th century, an abridgement of the divine office was made, but the result was not entirely happy, and it is hoped that the revision of the Chaldean breviary, carried out by the commission in 1938, may be adopted by the Malabarese.

Three liturgical books were published for the rite in the 18th century, which together form the *Takhsa:*

a) Ordo [104] *Chaldaicus Missae Beatorum Apostolorum, juxta ritum Ecclesiae Malabaricae.*

b) Ordo Chaldaicus Rituum et Lectionum, etc. [105]

c) Ordo Chaldaicus ministerii Sacramentorum Sanctorum. [106]

The general order [107] of the liturgy published in 1775 (1774) differs less from the Chaldean order than that which

---

[103] The revision of the ordination ceremonies will be undertaken first, and the other pontifical offices will follow later.

[104] Fol., Propaganda Press, Rome, 1774.

[105] Fol., *ibid.,* Rome 1775.

[106] Fol., *ibid.,* Rome, 1775.

[107] HANSSENS, *Instit. Lit. de Rit. Orient.,* t. II, part I, p. 505.

the fathers of the synod of Diamper produced by their corrections.

The editors were largely guided by a manuscript which had been prepared shortly before 1765 by Fr. Charles a S. Conrado.

Two documents [108] are extant, both dating from the time when a new missal was contemplated. One is a letter (January 8, 1767) from Cardinal Castelli, prefect of the Congregation of *Propaganda Fide,* to Mgr. Florentius, vicar apostolic in Malabar, and the other a document (January 28, 1768) in which are given the decisions of the commission [109] for the correction of the books of the Oriental church in regard to the Syro-Malabar rite. Cardinal Castelli alludes to the differences between the liturgy produced by Fr. Charles and Archbishop Menezes, and suggests that if difficulties concerning the rite arise in Malabar the book authorised by the synod of Diamper should be preferred to any other, unless the opposition should prove too great.

The commission on the liturgical books replied to four questions that had been put to them: *a)* Whether the prayer [110] when the priest goes up to the altar, which is found in the Chaldean and Diamper liturgies, should be said in "our" liturgy? The reply was *"Affirmative."* *b)* Whether the prayer said between the epistle and gospel ("O splendour of the Father's glory, and image of his *person*") should substitute the word "substance" for "person?" *"Nihil innovandum"* was the reply. *c)* Whether the commemoration of the pope should be made throughout the liturgy, and whether the hierarchy should be named as it is in the Chaldean rite?

---

[108] *Ibid.,* pp. 505-506.
[109] The decree of the commission is dated June 1, 1766.
[110] Prayer of the anthem of the sanctuary: "Before the glorious throne of thy greatness;" see Chaldean liturgy.

The response was "*Affirmative.*" *d*) Lastly, whether there should be an elevation of the host and chalice immediately after consecration, as has been lately introduced, since the normal oriental custom is to defer the elevation until a little before communion? The reply was again "*Affirmative.*"

With the single exception of the elevations at the consecration, it may be seen how closely the revisers wished to conform to eastern liturgical standards.

In regard to the 1775 (1774) edition of the missal, [111] the first part, that is between the trisagion and the great intercession, is the same as in the Chaldean Mass, with the exception of the recitation of the creed, which, as we have seen, is immediately after the gospel, instead of after the covering of the gifts. The second part closely follows the Mass of Menezes, with only two alterations. Thus, the second *lavabo*, which is found before the fraction in the Chaldean missal was omitted; and the second prayer, which is recited in the Chaldean rite during the fraction, together with the chant sung at the same time, are not after the second consecration, as in the Mass of Menezes, but they have been inserted after the consecration of the bread has been completed.

In this second part of the liturgy therefore the Mass of Menezes differs from the Chaldean rite a little less than the liturgy of 1775, although the 18th century book, at the end of the Mass, has prayers of inclination and also a blessing, which are in the Chaldean rite, but not in that of Menezes.

Another edition of the eucharistic liturgy was inserted in "*The Book of the Orders and the Lections... according*

[111] HANSSENS, *Ibid.*, p. 503.

to the Chaldean Order of Malabar," which was published in 1844 at Rome.

In 1912, the M.T.S. Press, Puttenpally, produced the Syriac liturgy with a Latin translation (*Ordo Missae Syro-Chaldaeo-Malabaricae cum translatione Latina*), which, with the exception of a *paroissien,* printed in 1917 by St. Joseph's Industrial School Press at Trinchinopoly, is the last edition of the Syro-Malabar rite, and is the text which has been given here.

A Comparison [112] *between the Malabar and Chaldean Rites.*

For the sake of convenience the points of difference between the Syro-Malabar rite and the parent Chaldean rite are compared in the following table:

a) The preparatory prayers before Mass, washing of the hands before the fraction, comminution (except the prayer and the proclamation of the deacon), and the distribution of blessed bread are omitted.

b) Communion under the species of bread only, except for the celebrant.

c) The priest vests at the beginning of the liturgy, immediately after washing his hands.

d) As in the Armenian rite, the creed is recited directly after the gospel, and therefore before the dismissal of the catechumens. In recent years, in Masses of an especially solemn character (*râzâ*), the creed has been restored to its proper position, that is after the dismissal of the catechumens and the rite of the entrance of the gifts.

e) All the prayers and ceremonies from the *kushápa* before the short intercession to the first prayer of the fraction have been inserted before the narration of the institu-

---

[112] HANSSENS, *Instit. Lit. de Rit. Orient.*, t. II, part I, pp. 389-390.

tion. The second prayer at the fraction is said immediately before the first part of the narration, and the first strophe of the hymn at the fraction follows it. The remaining part of this hymn is sung by the deacon after the formula which is recited at the fraction. Then the fraction is made.

f) The elevation is not made at the words "The holy thing to the holies is fitting in perfection," but with the prayer of introduction to the Lord's prayer, *more romano*. Two other elevations are made as in the Roman rite, after each part of the narration of the institution.

g) The laying of the hand of the deacon upon the chalice before the communion of the celebrant takes place, but in an abbreviated and altered rite.

h) The purification of the sacred vessels is carried out immediately after the paten has been replaced on the altar.

i) Some formulas have been taken from the Roman missal, such as those at the communion, both of the celebrant and the faithful.

j) The whole narration of the institution is found in the anaphora, and much of the wording is very similar to that in the Roman Mass.

A Mass of an especially solemn character is called *râzá*. [113] In addition to the deacon and subdeacon, there are two assistant priests in copes, which may be a survival of former concelebrating priests. Many of the prayers and ceremonies before the offertory at these solemn Masses are longer and different.

---

[113] Syriac, *râzâ*, plural *râzê*, "mystery." The term *râza* is used by the East Syrians for the liturgy, the eucharistic elements (even before consecration) or any rite of the Church, and by the Malabarese for an especially solemn liturgy.

31 - A. A. KING, *The Rites of Eastern Christendom* - 2nd Vol.

[65]

The Liturgy of the Apostles

The priest, after washing his hands, vests in the ordinary way, saying the Roman prayers, with the additional words for each prayer: "Father, Son and Holy Spirit for ever."

The deacon or server, carrying the missal, precedes the priest to the altar.

In plano, the celebrant gives up his biretta, bows, and says: "I will go unto the altar of God. To God, who giveth joy to my youth."

Then, ascending to the altar, the deacon puts the book on the missal-stand, while the priest places the chalice on the stone, and opens the book.

The priest and deacon return to the foot of the altar, where the priest continues: "I have entered into thy house, and I have worshipped before thy throne, O merciful Lord, pardon my faults and sins. In the name of the Father and of the Son and of the Holy Ghost. Amen. Holy, holy, holy is the Lord God of hosts. The heaven and the earth are full of his glory, and of the existence of his essence, and of the splendour of his glorious beauty, as saith the Lord: 'Heaven and earth are filled with me.' Praise be to thee, praise be to thee, praise be to thee, praise be to thy blessed Trinity, at all times, world without end. Amen."

The priest proceeds: "Your commandment" to which the deacon (server) responds: "The commandment of Christ."

In early days, it was the custom before Mass to ask permission of the bishop, and the formula of asking and giving

---

[114] In the translation of the Malabar Liturgy given by Neale and Littledale (*op. cit.*, p. 146), the rite begins at this point.

permission has become incorporated into the text of the liturgy.

Then in a clear voice, the priest says three times: "Glory [114] be to God in the highest," and three times the deacon (server) replies: "Amen."

The priest continues: "And on earth peace and good hope to men, at all times, world without end. Amen," and in the farced Lord's prayer which follows the deacon or server joins with the celebrant: "Our Father, who art in heaven, hallowed be thy name; thy kingdom come. Holy, holy, holy art thou. Our Father, who art in heaven, the heavens and the earth are full of the majesty of thy glory, and angels and men cry out to thee: Holy, holy, holy, art thou. Our Father, who art in heaven, hallowed be thy name; thy kingdom come; thy will be done on earth as it is in heaven. Give us this day bread of our necessity, forgive us our debts and our sins, as we also forgive our debtors; and lead us not into temptation, but deliver us from evil. For thine is the kingdom, power, and glory, for ever and ever. Amen."

The priest, bowing his head, continues: "Glory be to the Father, and to the Son, and to the Holy Ghost," and the deacon (server) answers: "From ever and for evermore. Amen. Amen."

A farced Lord's prayer is repeated by the celebrant and his minister: "Our Father, who art in heaven, hallowed be thy name; thy kingdom come. Holy, holy, holy, art thou, Our Father, who art in heaven, the heavens and earth are full of the majesty of thy glory, and angels and men cry out to thee: Holy, holy, holy, art thou!

The deacon now says: "Let us pray. Peace be with us."[115]

[115] It should be noted that in Syrian liturgies the priest says "with you," and the deacon "with us."

The priest continues: (on ordinary days) "Adored, glorified and honoured, praised, exalted and blessed. at all times, in heaven and on earth, be the adorable and glorious name of thy blessed Trinity, Lord of all, Father, Son and Holy Ghost, world without end. (Deacon or server) Amen."

(On Sundays and feasts) "Our Lord and our God, strengthen our weakness in thy mercy, that we may serve the sacred mysteries, which have been given for the renewal and salvation of our nature, through the mercy of thy well beloved Son, Lord of all, Father, Son and Holy Ghost for ever. (Deacon or server). Amen."

Three psalms—XIV (*Domine, quis habitabit*), CL (*Laudate Dominum in sanctis ejus*), CXVI (*Laudate Dominum omnes gentes*) — are recited alternately by the priest and deacon (server), with the following antiphon: "Make me stand, O Lord, with pure thoughts, before thy altar. Lord, who shall dwell in thy tabernacle? And who shall rest in thy holy hill?"

Then, ascending to the altar, the priest says: "How glorious and lovely is thy holy place, O God, the sanctifier of all things," and he kisses the altar.

When the deacon has said: "Peace be with us," he brings the thurible to the celebrant, who in a low voice blesses the incense: "In the name of thy most glorious Trinity, may this incense be blessed, which we place in thy honour, that it may be to thy good pleasure and to the remission of the debts of the sheep of thy flock, Father, Son and Holy Ghost, world without end. Amen." Three grains of incense are placed in the thurible.

The priest in a loud voice says: "For all thy helps and all the graces conferred upon us, which cannot be adequately repaid, we will praise thee and glorify thee, unceasingly, in thy triumphant Church, full of every help and happiness; for thou art the Lord and Creator of all things, Father, Son and Holy Ghost, world without end. (People, deacon or server): "Amen. We praise thee, Lord of all, we glorify thee, Jesus Christ, for thou art the renewer of our bodies and the good saviour of our souls."

The deacon or server continues: "I washed my hands clean, and encompassed thy altar, O Lord. We praise thee, Lord of all, we glorify thee, Jesus Christ; for thou art the renewer of our bodies and the good saviour of our souls." The dialogue still proceeds, with the priest saying: "Glory be to the Father and to the Son and to the Holy Ghost, for ever and for evermore. Amen. Amen. We praise thee, Lord of all."

Deacon (server): "And thee, Jesus Christ, we glorify."

Priest: "For thou art the renewer of our bodies."

Deacon (server): "And thou the good saviour of our souls. Let us pray. Peace be with us."

Priest: "In truth thou art, O Lord, the renewer of our bodies and the good saviour of our souls, and the perpetual guardian of our life. And thee, O Lord, we ought always to praise, adore and glorify, Lord of all, Father, Son and Holy Ghost, world without end."

Deacon (server): "Amen. Raise your voices, and praise, all ye people, the living God."

The trisagion is said in the following manner:

Priest: "Holy God, holy strong one, holy immortal one, have mercy on us. Glory be to the Father and to the Son and to the Holy Ghost."

Deacon (server): "Holy God, holy strong one, holy immortal one, have mercy on us, from ever and for evermore. Amen. Amen."

Priest: "Holy God."

Deacon (server): "Holy strong one."

Priest: "Holy immortal one."

Deacon (server): "Have mercy on us. Let us pray. Peace be with us."

Then, bowing to the cross, the priest at the epistle side prays with outstretched hands: (Sundays and feasts) "Enlighten, O Lord our God, the faculties of our thoughts that we may attend to and understand the sweet voice of thy life-giving and divine precepts; and grant that we may, through thy goodness and mercy, gather from them the fruits of love, hope and salvation, which may be profitable both to our soul and body; and that we may, ceaselessly and at all times, sing perpetual praise to thee, Lord of all, Father, Son and Holy Ghost, world without end. (Deacon or server). Amen."

(On others days) "O most wise ruler and most admirable cherisher of thy servants, and the great treasury, which in its goodness pours forth every help and every happiness, we beseech thee: Look upon us, O Lord, and be mindful of us, and have mercy on us, as thou art always accustomed, Lord of all, Father, Son and Holy Ghost, world without end. (Deacon or server) Amen."

The deacon (server), in preparation for the lesson, gives the monition: "Be silent," and the priest, with his hands on the book, announces the epistle: "My brethren, the Epistle of N.: Be pleased, Sir, to give thy blessing."

The priest, when the deacon (server) has responded: "May Christ bless thee," reads the epistle himself. This is concluded by "Praise be to Christ our Lord," said by the deacon (server).

Then, with hands joined before the breast, the priest prays silently: "O splendour of the Father's glory, and image of his *person*, [116] who manifested thyself in the body of our humanity, and illumined the darkness of our mind by the light of thy gospel, we praise thee, we adore thee, we glorify thee at all times, Lord of all, Father, Son and Holy Ghost, world without end."

The deacon or server, in a slavish copying of western ritual, moves the missal to the other side of the altar, and says: "Keep yourselves in silence and quiet."

The priest, bowing before the altar, says secretly: "Make me wise, O Lord, in thy law and enlighten our faculties through knowledge of thee; sanctify our souls by thy truth, that we may be always obedient to thy words and fulfil thy commandments, Lord of all, Father, Son and Holy Ghost, world without end."

Then, kissing the altar, the priest blesses the people: "Peace be with you," and the response is made: "And with thee and thy spirit."

The gospel is announced, and the priest signs the book and himself: "The holy Gospel of our Lord Jesus Christ, the preaching of *N.*" Deacon (server): "Glory be to Christ, our Lord."

Priest: "Be pleased, Sir, to give thy blessing."

Deacon (server): "May Christ bless thee."

The priest now chants the gospel, at the conclusion of which the deacon responds: "Glory be to Christ, our Lord;" while the priest, kissing the book, says: "To the eternal mercy which sent thee, O Christ, to us as the light of the world and the life of all, be glory for ever."

The creed normally follows immediately, as we have

---

[116] In answer to the query whether the word " person" should be changed to "substance," the commission within the Congregation of the Propagation of the Faith for the revision of the liturgical books replied *Nihil innovandum.* June 1, 1766.

seen, but, in the solemn liturgies known as *râzê*, it has been restored to its original position, after the dismissal of the catechumens and the ceremonies connected with the offertory.

The priest, extending and joining his hands, bows three times and says aloud: "We believe in one God." The conciliar "we" is the only variation from the creed in the Roman missal, and at the *Incarnatus* a genuflection is enjoined.

The diaconal litany, [117] which is said after the creed, is recited at a "low Mass" by the server: "Let us all stand rightly with joy [118] and cheerfulness and let us pray, saying: our Lord have mercy upon us."

After each clause, the people or the priest respond: "Our Lord, have mercy upon us."

Prayer is made for the hierarchy: "For the health of our holy Father Pope N., head of the entire Church of Christ, and of our Lord Bishop (Archbishop) N., and for all their subjects, we beseech thee."

The deacon or server, at the conclusion of the litany, brings the thurible to the priest for the blessing of the incense. The veil, paten, chalice and pall are each in turn held over the censer, [119] with the following prayers: (for the veil) "Lord our God, make this veil fragrant, like the veil of Elias the true prophet. In the name of the Father and of the Son and of the Holy Ghost." (for the paten) "Lord our God, make this paten fragrant, like the paten of Aaron, the excellent priest, in the tabernacle of the covenant. In the name of the Father and of the Son and of the Holy Ghost." (for the chalice) " Lord our God, make this chalice fragrant, like the chalice of Aaron, the excellent priest, in

[117] Cf. Ambrosian and Byzantine rites.
[118] On ferial days: " with repentance and earnestness."
[119] Cf. Maronite rite.

the tabernacle of the covenant, Lord of fragrant roots and sweet-smelling aromatics. In the name of the Father and of the Son and of the Holy Ghost." (for the pall) "Lord our God, make this pall fragrant. In the name of the Father and of the Son and of the Holy Ghost."

The priest, going to the left corner of the altar, then pours wine crosswise into the chalice, saying: "The precious blood is poured into the chalice of Christ our Lord. In the name of the Father and of the Son and of the Holy Ghost."

The synod of Diamper [120] ordered the word "wine" to be substituted for "precious blood," but the missal of 1912 and the *paroissien* of 1917 have both reverted to the original wording.

Adding a little water, the priest says: "Then came one of the soldiers and pierced with a lance the side of our Lord, and immediately there came out blood and water, and he that saw it gave testimony and his testimony is true. [121] In the name of the Father and of the Son and of the Holy Ghost."

Then, pouring wine a second time into the chalice: "The wine is mixed with the water, and the water with the wine. In the name of the Father and of the Son and of the Holy Ghost."

The supplication is now said by the deacon (server): "Through prayer and supplication, the angel of peace and mercy we ask ," etc, the priest responding to each clause: "From thee, O Lord." The fifth and last petition: "Let us commend our souls and the soul of each one of us to the Father and the Son and the Holy Ghost," has the reply: "To thee, O Lord our God."

[120] Act V, decree I.
[121] Cf. St. John XIX, 34, 35

The priest, in the meanwhile, [122] having covered the
chalice and placed it near the stone on the left side, goes
to the right, where he sets the host on the paten, with the
following prayer: "This paten is signed with the sacred
body of our Lord Jesus Christ. In the name of the Father
and of the Son and of the Holy Ghost."

The supplication finished, the priest, in the middle of
the altar, says, with outstretched hands: "Lord God powerful, we beseech and implore thee: perfect in us thy grace,
and pour forth through our hands thy gifts and thy mercy
and the goodness of thy Godhead that they may effect the
forgiveness of the debts of thy people, and the remission of
the sins of all the sheep of thy flock, whom in thy grace and
mercy thou hast chosen for thyself, Lord of all, Father, Son
and Holy Ghost."

The people (server) respond: "Amen," and the deacon
(server) continues: "Be pleased, Father, to give thy blessing. Bow down yours heads for the imposition of hands, and
receive the blessing."

Then the priest, bowing down over the altar, says in a
low voice: "Lord God powerful, Lord God powerful, thine
is the holy Catholic Church. For the sheep of thy flock
have been purchased by the wonderful passion of thy Christ,
and through the grace of the Holy Ghost, who is consub-
stantial with thee in thy glorious Godhead, are conferred
the orders of the true priesthood by the imposition of hands.
Through thy mercy, O Lord, thou didst render the littleness
of our weak nature worthy in order that we may become
recognised members in the great body of the Catholic
Church for the dispensation of spiritual helps to the souls
of the faithful. Do thou therefore, O Lord, perfect in us

[122] "after this," paroissien of 1917.

thy grace and pour forth thy gifts through our hands; and may thy mercy and the goodness of thy divinity be upon us and upon this people whom thou didst elect."

Extending his hands and raising his voice, the priest continues: "Grant, O Lord, in thy goodness, that all the days of our life we may, every one of us equally, please thy Godhead by good works of justice which appease and reconcile the adorable will of thy clemency, and that we may be made worthy, by the help of thy grace, to offer thee always glory and honour, praise and worship, Lord of all, Father, Son and Holy Ghost. (Deacon or server) Amen."

The dismissal of the catechumens follows.

Priest and deacon (server): "Who hath not received baptism, let him leave."

Priest: "Who hath not put on the sign of life, let him leave."

Deacon or server: "Who hath not received it, [123] let him leave."

Priest: "Go, hearers, and watch the doors."

Liturgy of the Faithful

The deacon (server) now says: "Let us pray. Peace be with us," and the priest goes to the right side of the altar, where, taking the paten with the host in both hands, he raises it to the level of the forehead.

Then, returning to the centre, the celebrant turns to the people, and says: "With expectation I have waited for the Lord, with expectation I have waited for the Lord. With fear and love [124] let us all offer to him, upon the holy altar, the body of Christ and his most precious blood, [125] and with angels let us cry out to him: Holy, holy, holy Lord God."

[123] See Chaldean rite.

The deacon (server) responds: "The poor shall eat and be filled. With fear and love," etc.

Then, the deacon having said "Let us pray," the priest takes the chalice in his right hand and the paten in his left, and, holding his arms cross-wise, says in a low voice: "We will offer glory to thy most blessed Trinity, always and for ever. May Christ, who was immolated for our salvation, and commanded us to celebrate the memory of his passion, death, burial and resurrection, accept this sacrifice from our hands, through his grace and mercy, world without end. Amen."

The offerings are replaced on the altar, and the base of the chalice is three times touched with the paten.

The celebrant continues: "Disposed, disposed, disposed and arranged are these holy mysteries—glorious, life-giving and divine—on the sacred altar of Christ, until his glorious second advent from heaven. To him be glory and praise, worship and honour, now and always, world without end. (Deacon or server) Amen."

Covering the mysteries with the veil, the priest says aloud:

"Glory be to the Father and to the Son and to the Holy Ghost. Upon the sacred altar let there be a commemoration of the Virgin Mary, Mother of God."

The deacon responds: "From ever and for evermore. Amen, Amen. Pray ye, apostles of the Son and the friends of the Only-begotten, that there may be peace upon every creature."

The dialogue is continued.

---

[124] " trembling," *paroissien* of 1917.
[125] The synod of Diamper had substituted the words " holy bread" and " precious chalice."

Priest: "Let all the people say: Amen, amen. Let us celebrate upon the altar the memory of St. Thomas, in company with the just who have triumphed and the martyrs who have been crowned with glory."

Deacon (server): "The Lord mighty is with us, our King with us, angels with us, as also our helper the God of Jacob."

Priest: "The little in company with the great, behold, all the dead have fallen asleep in thy hope, and them whom thou wouldst through thy resurrection raise up again in glory."

Deacon (server): "Pour forth your hearts before him. By fasting, prayer and contrition of heart we shall appease Christ and his Father and his Spirit."

The priest, at the left side of the altar, washes his hands, saying: "May God, the Lord of all, remove the uncleanness of our debts and our offences in the immense ocean of his mercy. Amen."

Then, wiping them, he continues: "May the Lord wipe away the defilement of our sins through his grace and mercy. Amen."

The priest, from the middle of the altar, now blesses the deacon (server): "May God, the Lord of all, give thee strength to sing his praises," and the deacon responds with a prayer for the living and dead: "Let us pray. Peace be with us. Pray for the memory of the Catholic fathers and bishops, of all priests and deacons, of unmarried youths and virgins, of all our fathers and brothers, of all our sons and daughters, of all faithful kings that love Christ, of all who have died and departed from this world in the true faith, of all prophets and apostles and of all martyrs and confessors of this place and of all other places. May God, who will crown them in the resurrection from the dead, grant us good hope and portion with them, and life and inheritance in the kingdom of heaven. Be pleased, Father, to give thy blessing. May this oblation be graciously accepted and may it be sanctified by the power of God the Father, the Son and the Holy Ghost, that it may through the grace of Christ avail for our help, our salvation and life everlasting in the kingdom of heaven."

In the meanwhile, the priest, having kissed the altar in the centre, to the right, to the left, and again in the centre, says, in a low voice, the following prayer: "I give thee thanks, my Father, Lord of heaven and earth, Father, Son and Holy Ghost (repeated); for, whilst I was yet a sinner, thou didst make me worthy, by thy grace, to offer in thy presence these holy mysteries—glorious, life-giving and divine—of the body and blood of thy Christ, that I may dispense them to thy people and the sheep of thy flock, in satisfaction for their debts, for the remission of their sins, for the salvation of their souls, for the reconciliation of the entire world, and for the peace and tranquillity of all churches."

Then, kissing the altar in the centre and to the right, the priest, looking towards the gospel side, makes the sign of the cross and says: "Be pleased, Lord, to give thy blessing: Brethren, pray for me that this oblation may be perfected through my hands."

The deacon responds: "May God, the Lord of all, give thee strength to sing his praises."

The priest, again kissing the altar, continues: "I give thee thanks, my Father."

Looking towards the epistle side, the priest now repeats the prayers and ceremonies, and the deacon gives the same response.

Then the priest, kissing the altar and joining his hands

on his breast, says: "O Lord our God, O Lord our God, regard not the multitude of our sins, and let not thy majesty turn away with disgust from the weight of our evil, but through thy ineffable grace sanctify this sacrifice, and impart to it the virtue and power to remit our many sins, so that when thou, our Lord Jesus Christ, shalt manifest thyself at the end of time in that humanity which thou didst receive from us, we may find in thy sight grace and mercy and be made worthy to sing thy praises with the hosts of angels."

The altar is again kissed, and the priest, bowing down, recites in a low voice the "first prayer of the apostles:" "We acknowledge, O Lord our God, the abundant riches of thy grace to us (repeated); for, whilst we were full of sin and weakness, through the multitude of thy mercy thou didst make us worthy to be the ministers of the sacred mysteries of the body and blood of thy Christ; and we implore thy help for the strengthening of our souls, that we may in perfect charity and true faith dispense the gifts which thou hast conferred upon us" (he kisses the altar, and repeats "that we may in perfect charity" etc.).

Then, aloud and with hands placed cross-wise on his breast, the priest says: "And offer thee glory and honour, praise and worship, now and always, world without end. (Deacon or server) Amen."

When the people have been blessed: "Peace be with you," and the answer given: "And with thy spirit," the deacon, if it be a solemn liturgy, says: "My brethren, give the peace to one another in the love of Christ," and the *pax* is given.

The deacon or server now calls for the people's prayers and attention in a long bidding: "For all patriarchs, bishops, priests and deacons; for all classes of those who by death have departed from the society of the Church, and for the living; for the peace of the world and for the crowning of the year that it may be blessed and filled with abundance through thy goodness; for the entire progeny of the Church that they may be found worthy to receive of this offering in thy sight; for all thy servants and handmaids, who at this time stand before thee, and for all men, and for all of us, may this oblation be accepted for ever. Amen. Let us all confess, and ask and implore the Lord with pure minds and with sighs. Stand with due reverence, and attend to the things which are performed—to the tremendous mysteries which are consecrated. The priest (pontiff) has already begun to pray that through his intercession peace may be multiplied in you. Cast down your eyes and lift up your minds to heaven. With vigilance and earnestness pray and beseech at this time; let no one dare to speak; let him who prays pray in his heart: remain in silence and in fear and be praying. Peace be with us."

The priest, in the meanwhile, recites the following prayer: "Lord God powerful, help my infirmity in thy mercy, and by the aid of thy grace make me worthy to offer in thy sight this holy and living sacrifice, for the benefit of the whole congregation and for the glory of thy most blessed Trinity, Father, Son and Holy Ghost, world without end. Amen."

The deacon (server) responds: "With vigilance and earnestness."

The veil is now removed from the offerings, and incense is blessed.

The priest says in a clear voice: "The grace of our Lord Jesus Christ, the charity of God the Father, and the communication of the Holy Ghost be with us all, now ✝ and always, world without end" (he kisses the altar). The deacon or server answers "Amen."

Anaphora

Priest: "Lift up your hearts" (he kisses the altar on the right side).

Deacon (server): "Towards thee, God of Abraham and Isaac and Israel, O King of glory."

Priest: "The sacrifice is offered to God, the Lord of all" (he kisses the altar on the left side).

Deacon (server): "It is meet and just. Peace be with us."

The priest continues: "Lord, Lord, give us a trustful countenance in thy sight, that we may go through these living and holy mysteries with confidence and with consciences free from every stain and evil, from envy, deceit and harshness. Implant in us, O Lord, chastity and concord with each other and with all men. Be pleased, Lord, to give thy blessing (thrice repeated): Brethren, pray for me," etc.

The deacon (server) responds: "May Christ hear thy prayers, may Christ accept thy offering, may Christ glorify thy priesthood in the kingdom of heaven. May he be well pleased with this sacrifice which thou offerest [126] for thyself, for us, and for the whole world, which hopes and looks for the grace of Christ and his mercy for ever. Amen."

The priest, with extended hands, says: "The adorable and glorious name of the most blessed Trinity, Father, Son and Holy Ghost, who created the world in his goodness, and its dwellers in his mercy, and did great favour to mortal men, is worthy of glory from all mouths, of praise from all tongues, and of worship and exaltation from all creatures. Thousands upon thousands, and myriads upon myriads of

[126] The synod of Diamper had ordered the following substitution: " which thou offerest for thyself, for us and for the whole Catholic Church and for all orthodox worshippers of the Catholic and Apostolic faith."

32 - A. A. KING, The Rites of Eastern Christendom - 2nd Vol.

angels, prostrate themselves and adore thy majesty; and the host of supernal ministers of fire and spirit glorify thy name, and with holy cherubim and heavenly seraphim they offer worship to thy majesty."

Here the priest kisses the altar, and raising and joining his hands, says in a clear voice: "Crying out and glorifying without ceasing, and proclaiming to one another and saying."

The deacon (server) then continues: "Holy, holy holy (bell is rung) is the Lord God of hosts; the heavens and the earth are full of his glory. Hosanna in the highest. Hosanna to the Son of David. Blessed is he that came and is to come in the name of the Lord. Hosanna in the highest."

The priest, in the meanwhile, says: "Holy art thou, O God, the only true Father from whom all paternity in heaven and earth is named (he kisses the altar in the middle). Holy art thou, O eternal Son, by whom all things were created (he kisses the right side of the altar). Holy art thou, Holy Ghost, the principle by which all things are sanctified" (he kisses the left side of the altar).

The Malabarese rite differs from that of the Chaldean, in that all the prayers from the *kushápa* before the short intercession to the first prayer of the fraction have been placed before the narrative of the institution; while another prayer of the fraction is said immediately after the first part of the narrative.

The first verse of the hymn of the fraction follows, but the other verses are sung by the deacon after the formula of the fraction.

The priest, striking his breast, now says a *kushápa*: [127] "Woe to me, woe to me; for I am stupified seeing that I

[127] Second *kushápa* in the chaldean rite.

am a man of unclean lips and live in the midst of people whose lips are unclean. My eyes have beheld the King, the Lord of hosts. How terrible is this place. For this day I have been seen face to face by the Lord, and this is none other than the house of God. May thy goodness be upon us now, O Lord; purify our uncleanness and make our lips holy. Blend, O Lord, the voice of our weakness with the praises of the seraphim and the archangels. Glory be to thy mercy, which united earthly men in fellowship with heavenly spirits."

Then, kissing the altar in the middle, he continues: "Be pleased, Lord, to give thy blessing (thrice repeated); brethren, pray for me that this oblation may be perfected through my hands."

The deacon (server) responds: "May Christ hear," etc., and the priest, in a low voice, says: "And with these celestial hosts we praise thee, O Lord (repeated): we, also, thy weak and frail and miserable servants. For thou hast done us a great favour, which cannot be repaid, by clothing thyself with our humanity, that it may be vivified by thy divinity; by exalting our lowliness, by elevating our fallen nature, by endowing our mortality with life, by forgiving us our debts, and by making us, sinners, justified before thee, by enlightening our knowledge; by condemning, O Lord our God, our enemies, and by rendering the littleness of our weak nature victorious through the abundant mercy of thy grace. For all thy helps, therefore, and for all the graces conferred upon us, we will render thee glory, honour, praise and worship, now † (he kisses the altar) and always, world without end."

The deacon (server) responds: "Amen. Pray with your hearts. Peace be with us."

Neale [128] and Littledale in their version of the Malabar liturgy appear to have invented a place for the narrative of the institution, as it was unthinkable to them that the epiclesis should precede it; while, on grounds of Anglican theology, it was necessary to supply the deficiency of the anaphora of the Apostles. Thus, it has been given by them in this position, after a further prayer: "Glory to thy holy name, and adoration to thy divinity, ..."

In the Catholic rite, the priest now says in a low voice: "Lord God of hosts, mercifully hear the voice of my cry, who now stands before thee. Attend, O Lord, and hear my sighs, with which I sigh before thy majesty; receive the prayer of me, a sinner, by which I ask thy grace at this hour when the sacrifice is being offered up to thy Father. Have mercy on all creatures, forgive all debtors, bring back the erring, cheer up the afflicted, pacify the agitated, heal the sick, console them that are in tribulation, and fill up the alms of those that work justice for thy name's sake. Be merciful to me also, a sinner, through thy grace. Lord God of hosts, receive this oblation on behalf of the Supreme Pontiff of Rome N., the head and ruler of the entire world, and for

---

[128] "I have ventured to make a considerable alteration in the order of the above prayers. As we have the Malabar Liturgy from the Portuguese revisers, the sequence of the collects is that which is given by bracketed numerals in the margin. Here the invocation of the Holy Ghost, contrary to the use of every other oriental liturgy, preceded the words of Institution. This, in itself, would be a sufficient proof that an alteration had been made; though very carelessly, if not *mala fide*, no notice is given of it. But fortunately the Nestorian Liturgy of Theodore the Interpreter bears a sufficient resemblance to this to shew what was the original order: *I have therefore arranged the prayers according to that.* The Liturgy of All Apostles... bears, as would be natural, a closer resemblance still to the Malabar; but as All Apostles, from whatever cause, has not the words of Institution at all, it is not so useful in shewing how the Malabar was arranged." *Op. cit.*, p. 165, n. 14.

Bishop N., who now presides over our people; for the holy
Catholic Church, for all priests, kings and princes; for the
honour of all prophets, apostles, martyrs and confessors;
for the just and holy fathers who were pleasing in thy sight;
for all those who mourn and are in trouble, for all the poor
and the oppressed, for all those that are sick and in suffering; for all the dead who in thy name have gone and are
departed from our midst; and for all this people who hope
and look for thy mercy, and lastly for me who am so weak,
poor and miserable. Lord our God, Lord our God, according to thy goodness and the multitude of thy mercies; visit
thy people and me thy miserable servant; consider not my
sins and faults; but by thy grace make us worthy to receive
forgiveness of our debts and the remission of our sins, by
the merits of the sacred body which we receive in true faith.
Amen. Be pleased, Lord, to give thy blessing," etc. (repeated thrice).

The deacon says: "May Christ hear thy prayers," etc.,
and the priest, bowing down over the altar, continues:
"Accept, O Lord, through thy great and ineffable mercy
(repeated), accept the salutary and well-pleasing commemoration of the Virgin Mary, Mother of God, of all the just
and holy fathers who pleased thee by celebrating the memory
of the body and blood of thy Christ, whom we offer thee
upon thy altar, pure and holy, according as thou hast taught
us to do. Grant us peace and tranquillity all the days of
the world, so that all the dwellers on the earth may know
thee, that thou art God the only true Father and that thou
didst send our Lord Jesus Christ thy well-beloved Son.
And he, our Lord and our God, came and taught us, by
his life-giving preaching, all the purity and holiness of the
prophets and the apostles, of the martyrs and the confessors,
of doctors and bishops, of priests and deacons, and of all

the sons of the holy Catholic Church who have been marked (he makes the sign of the cross with his right thumb on the altar) with the living and life-giving seal of holy baptism. And to us also, O Lord (repeated thrice), thy weak, miserable and poor servants, who have assembled in thy name and stand at this hour in thy presence, has thy example come down by tradition. With joy and exultation, therefore, we venerate thy memory and go through these mysteries—great, awe-inspiring and lifegiving—of the passion, death, burial and resurrection of our Lord and Saviour Jesus Christ."

The position of the epiclesis, before the narrative of the institution, has given rise to much controversy, but it was *not* the synod of Diamper that effected the change.

Menezes appears to have contented himself with the addition of "*filii*" after "*Christi*," and not to have tampered with the epiclesis properly so-called.

In that case, it may well be that the invocation was moved here by the Malabarese themselves, in the same way as they effected other changes.

The priest, spreading his hands over the mysteries, says: "Let, therefore, O Lord, thy Holy Spirit come down."

The deacon (server) responds: "In silence and in fear remain and pray. Peace be with us."

Then the priest continues: "And may he rest upon this oblation of thy servant, and may he bless it and make it holy, that it may be to us, O Lord, unto the forgiveness of debts and the remission of sins, and unto the great hope of resurrection from the dead and the new life in the kingdom of heaven with all those who were pleasing in thy sight. For all this great and admirable dispensation towards us we give thee thanks and we unceasingly glorify thee, publicly and with a trustful countenance, in thy church, redeemed

with the precious blood of thy Christ, in thy church, redeemed with the precious blood of thy Christ: (*qanona*) offering glory and honour, thanks and worship to thy living,
holy and vivifying name, now † and always, world without
end (he kisses the altar on the left side). (Deacon or server): Amen."

The priest, bowing his head and joining his hands, says:
"O Christ, the peace of those in heaven and the great hope
of those on earth: establish, O Lord, thy peace in the four
quarters of the world and especially in the holy Catholic
Church; grant accord between the priesthood and the
rulers; ward off wars from the ends of the earth; disperse
the nations divided amongst themselves and who desire
wars, that we may live a calm and peaceful life, in all so-
briety and fear of God. Not to us, O Lord, not to us, but
to thy name give the glory (he joins his hands on his breast).
Have mercy [129] on me, O God, according to thy great mercy.
And according to the multitude of thy tender mercies blot
out my sins. For I know my iniquities, and my sins are
always before me. To thee only have I sinned, and have
done evil before thee: that thou mayest be justified in thy
word and mayest overcome in thy judgments. For I was
conceived in iniquity, and in sin did my mother conceive
me. Behold thou hast loved truth, and the hidden things
of thy wisdom thou hast made manifest to me. Sprinkle
me with hyssop and I shall be cleansed. To thee have I
raised my eyes, [130] O dweller of heaven: as the eyes of
servants towards their masters, and as the eyes of the hand-
maid towards her mistress, so are our eyes turned to thee,

[129] Psalm L, 1-9.
[130] Psalm CXXII, 1-3.

O Lord our God, until thou shalt show mercy to us. Have mercy on us, O Lord, have mercy on us."

The deacon (server) brings the thurible for the blessing of the incense, and the priest says: "May our prayer be fragrant before thee, O Lord our God, and the incense, too, of our censer: like the censer of Aaron the excellent priest in the tabernacle of the covenant, O Lord of roots breathing odour and of sweet-smelling aromatics, Father, Son and Holy Ghost, world without end. Amen."

Then, extending and folding his hands on his breast, the priest is censed, saying three times: "Make fragrant, O Lord our God, the foulness of our impurity and our corruption by the sweet odour of thy charity, and purify me by its virtue from the uncleanness of sin; O good pastor, who came forth in quest of us and found us out being lost, forgive me my debts and the sins which I have committed knowingly and in ignorance."

At the censing of the deacon (server): "O Lord our God, make this servant acceptable, who stands before thy holy and excellent altar."

Upon the people: "O Lord our God, make this people acceptable, who look and hope for thy mercy."

Upon the altar: "O Lord our God, make fragrant this altar, erected in the likeness of the sepulchre of our Lord, and his throne and his body and blood of propitiation."

Upon the mysteries: "Be pleased, Lord, to give thy blessing (repeated three times). May the mercy of thy grace bring us to these holy mysteries—glorious, life-giving and divine—although we are unworthy, although in truth we are unworthy" (repeated thrice, each time kissing the altar).

The synod of Diamper, as we have seen, was not responsible for placing the narrative of the institution at the fraction, but it appears to have been the work of a Chaldean bishop earlier in the century. Thus, the formula [131] in the text of the Mass annexed to the *acta* of the synod is extant, showing that it was not derived immediately from the Latin rite, for, although *"calix sanguinis mei"* is Roman, it is also found in various Maronite anaphoras. [132] Certain verbal changes were made by the synod, and the Portuguese [133] appeared to have been under the impression that such words as *"enim," "aeterni,"* and *"mysterium fidei"* had been used by our Lord at the last supper.

The consecration begins with the priest joining his hands and saying in a low voice: "Glory be to thy holy name, O Lord Jesus Christ, and worship to thy majesty, always, world without end. Amen."

Then, wiping his thumbs and index fingers on the corporal, the priest continues: "Who the day before his passion took bread (he takes the host) into his holy and venerable hands and with his eyes lifted up towards heaven (he raises his eyes to heaven), unto thee O God, his almighty Father, giving thanks to thee (he bows his head) did bless †††,

---

[131] *" Gloria nomini tuo sancto... vivunt in aeternum. Dominus noster Jesus Christus in illa nocte qua tradebatur accepit panem hunc sanctum in sanctas ac puras manus suas et elevavit oculos suos in coelum et gratias egit Deo Patri omnium rerum creatori et benedixit ac fregit deditque discipulis suis et dixit: Accipite et comedite ex hoc pane omnes vos, hoc est in veritate corpus meum. Similiter postquam coenavit accepit hunc calicem manibus suis puris et gratias egit et benedixit et dedit discipulis suis dicens: Accipite et bibite omnes vos ex hoc calice, quotiescumque enim comederitis panem hunc et biberitis hunc calicem mei memoriam recoletis. Hic est in veritate calix sanguinis mei qui pro vobis et pro multis effundetur in debitorum propitiationem et in peccatorum remissionem, et hoc erit vobis pignus in saecula saeculorum."*

[132] e. g. St. Xystus (RENAUDOT, *op. cit.* II, 136); Peter II (*Ibid.*, II, 156); St. John Evangelist (*Ibid.*, II, 164).

[133] "The Roman Church," says the synod, "taught from apostolic tradition that Christ pronounced these words," and the reference is to *all* the words used at the consecration.

break, and give to his disciples saying: "Take, and eat ye all of this; for this is my body."

The priest adores the sacred host and shows it to the people, as he says: "Behold the living and life-giving bread which came down from heaven, and gives life to all the world. Those who eat it shall not die; those who receive it shall be saved and sanctified, and by it live for ever."

Then, replacing the host on the paten, he again adores.

This prayer [134] is said at the fraction in the Chaldean rite; while the liturgy published by Archbishop Menezes places it after the *second* consecration.

The priest proceeds: "In like manner, after they had supped (he takes the chalice) taking also this excellent chalice into his holy and venerable hands, giving thee thanks (he bows) he blessed †††, and gave to his disciples saying: Take and drink ye all of this; For this is the chalice of my blood of the new and eternal testament (the mystery of faith) which is shed for you and for many unto the re-mission of sin (he adores and elevates the chalice). As often as ye do these things ye shall do them in remembrance of me."

The 1912 missal directs the deacon (server), after the elevation of the host, to say: "I am the bread of life which came down from heaven; I am the bread which came down from on high, said our Saviour, in mystery, to his disciples; all, who approach me with love and receive me, will live for ever in me, and possess the kingdom as an inheritance."

The celebrant, as in the Roman rite, is required after the consecration to keep his first fingers and thumbs joined.

The priest, with outstretched hands, continues: "Glory

[134] Hanssens (*Instit. Lit. de Rit. Orient.* t. II, part I, p. 502) says that the synod of Diamper enjoined the prayer to be said, not after the first consecration, but only after the second consecration and elevation.

be to thee, O Lord (thrice repeated), for thy ineffable gift to us, world without end."

Then the deacon (server) sings: "His ministers that do his will—the cherubim, the seraphim and the archangels—stand with fear and trembling before the altar, and watch the priest (pontiff) who breaks and divides the body of Christ unto the forgiveness of debts. Open to me, O good Lord, the gates of justice, for thy doorway is always open to the penitent, and thou callest sinners to draw nigh to thee. Open to us, O Lord, the gates of thy tender mercy, that we may enter them and sing thy praises day and night."

The priest, in the meanwhile, performs the fraction, a ceremony which so unaccountably raised the ire [135] of the Portuguese at the synod of Diamper [136] (1599).

The celebrant genuflects and says: "We draw near, O Lord, with true faith in thy name, to these holy mysteries; and through thy grace we break, and through thy mercy we sign, the body and blood of thy well-beloved Son, our Lord Jesus Christ, in the name of the Father and of the Son and of the Holy Ghost."

---

[135] Cf. Pope St. Zachary (741-752) and the pontifical blessings before communion in the Gallican rite.

[136] "*Cum in Syriacis istius Episcopatus Missalibus praescripta reperiatur impia quaedam et sacrilega caeremonia...: scilicet quo secundum absurdam opinionem suam, sanguis corpus penetret, et ita sanguis corpori coniungatur: quae opinio ad haeresim Nestorii et eius sequacium relationem habet. Impie si quidem affirmant, sub specie panis esse solum corpus Christi absque sanguine; et sub specie vini, sanguinem sine corpore. Idcirco mandat sancta synodus in virtute sanctae obedientiae, et sub poena excommunicationis ipso facto incurrendae, ut nullus cacanar, sive sacerdos, talem caeremoniam observare audeat, utque illa ex Missalibus deleatur: eo quod innuat talem haeresim, et praeterea inscitiam continet, quod existiment a speciebus penetrationem esse ad corpus et sanguinem Christi.*" There seems, however, no evidence to show that the Malabarese by the ceremony of the fraction denied the doctrine of concomitance, and the usage has been retained.

The priest breaks the host in two and, placing that half which is in his left hand on the paten (not placed as before, but in a different way), he signs the chalice with the other half from east to west and from north to south, touching about a third of the particle, and sprinkling it with the precious blood.

The priest, as the chalice is signed, says: "The precious blood is signed with the life-giving body of our Lord Jesus Christ, in the name of the Father and of the Son and of the Holy Ghost."

Then, signing the half on the paten with the half in his right hand, he continues: "The sacred body is signed with the propitiatory blood of our Lord Jesus Christ, in the name of the Father and of the Son and of the Holy Ghost."

He joins the two halves of the host above the chalice, saying: "Divided and sanctified, perfected and consummated, conjoined and commixed together are these holy mysteries—glorious, life-giving and divine—in the adorable and exalted name of the most glorious Trinity of the Father, Son and Holy Ghost, that they may be to us, O Lord, unto the forgiveness of debts and the remission of sins, unto the great hope of resurrection from the dead and the new life in the kingdom of heaven;—to us and the holy Catholic Church of Christ our Lord, here and in all places, now and always, world without end. Amen."

Before the last words of this prayer, the priest places the two halves of the host on the paten, one upon the other in the form of a cross, so that the lower half is turned towards the chalice and the upper half towards the priest.

Then, wiping his fingers over the chalice, he genuflects, signs himself on the forehead, blesses the assistants, and unfolds the veil spread over the mysteries.

The priest, with outstretched hands and in a low voice,

says: "Glory be to thee, our Lord Jesus Christ, for, whilst I was unworthy, thou didst appoint me by thy grace as the minister and mediator of thy holy mysteries —glorious, life-giving and divine. By the grace of thy kindness make me worthy of the forgiveness of debts and the remission of sins. Amen."

Joining his hands and in a loud voice, the priest continues with a *qanona:* "The grace of our Lord Jesus Christ, the charity of God the Father, and the communication of the Holy Ghost, be with us all, now and always, world without end †. (Deacon or server) Amen."

Then, again in a low voice, he proceeds: "Blessed art thou, O Lord God of our fathers, and exalted is thy name for ever. For thou didst deal with us not according to our sins; but according to the multitude of thy tender mercies; thou didst liberate us from the power of darkness and invite us into the kingdom of thy well-beloved Son, our Lord Jesus Christ."

This is followed by the deprecatory "Hymn of St. James" (of Nisibis): "O Father of truth, behold thy Son, the victim which reconciles thee. Do thou accept him, who died for me, and by him I shall be made just. Receive this oblation from my hands and be appeased towards me: remember not my sins, the sins I committed before thy majesty. Behold, his blood, which was shed on Calvary for my salvation, pleads for me. Accept my prayer for his sake. If thou were to weigh the multitude of my sins, and the multitude of thy mercies, thy mercies would greatly outweigh the mountains thou hast suspended. Look on my sins, and look, also, on the holocaust in atonement for them. For, the holocaust and the victim are far greater than the debts. For my sins did thy well-beloved Son endure the nails and the lance, and his passion is sufficient to appease

thee, and make me live again by its merits. Glory be to
the Father who sent his Son for our sake; worship to the
Son who, by his death on the cross, redeemed the world;
and thanksgiving to the Holy Ghost by whom the mystery
of our redemption was consummated. Blessed is he who
in his charity gave life to us all; to him be glory."

The deacon (server)), in the meanwhile, says: "With fear
and respect let us all approach the mysteries of the precious
body and blood of our Saviour, in the purity of our hearts
and in the true faith. Let us recall to our minds his passion,
and contemplate his resurrection. For our sake did the
only-begotten of God receive from us men a mortal body
with a rational and spiritual soul endowed with immortality.
By his laws he gave us life, and by his precepts he led us
from error into the knowledge of truth. After all the dispensation of redemption, undertaken for us, was fulfilled,
the first-fruits of our nature endured the cross, and he rose
from the dead, and ascended into heaven, handing over to
us his holy mysteries by which we may keep in remembrance
all his mercy towards us. Let us therefore with overflow-
ing charity and a humble heart receive the gift of eternal
life, and through holy prayer and deep contrition participate
in the mysteries of the Church. With the hope of penance
let us convert ourselves from our iniquities and weep over
our sins, and ask mercy and pardon from God, the Lord
of all, and let us forgive our companions their offences."

The people [137] five times repeat: "Lord, forgive our
sins and the offences of thy servants," while the deacon
(server) makes the following responses: 1) "And let us
make our consciences free from dissensions and conten-
tions." 2) "Purifying our souls from anger and enmity."

[137] Priest in a " low Mass."

3) "Let us receive the oblation, and may we be sanctified by the Holy Ghost." 4) "In the unity and concord of our minds let us receive in mutual harmony the participation of mysteries." 5) "That they may be to us, O Lord, unto the resurrection of our bodies and the salvation of our souls."

Finally, the people (priest) say: "And unto life everlasting. Amen."

The priest, when the deacon (server) has said: "Let us pray. Peace be with us," continues in a low voice: "Pardon thou, Lord, through thy mercy, the sins and offences of thy servants, and sanctify our lips by thy grace that we may, with all the saints in thy heavenly kingdom, bring forth to thy exalted divinity the fruits of glory."

This is followed by a form of the *agnus Dei:* "Lamb of the living God, who taketh away the sins of the world." (Deacon or server): "Spare us, O Lord."

"Lamb of the living God, who taketh away the sins of the world." (Deacon or server): "Graciously hear us, O Lord."

"Lamb of the living God, who taketh away the sins of the world." (Deacon or server): "Have mercy on us."

The priest, genuflecting, now elevates the host and chalice together, with the host in his right hand and the chalice under it, in his left.

Then, again genuflecting, he says aloud: "Make us worthy, O Lord our God, that we may always stand before thee without blemish, with pure heart and a trustful countenance, and with that confidence which by thy mercy thou hast conferred upon us. We will all together invoke thee and say thus."

The people (server) respond with the Lord's prayer, and, as an embolism, the priest, says in a low voice: "Lord

God powerful, our good God and our Father full of mercy, we ask and implore thee for the clemency of thy grace. Lead us not, O Lord, into temptation, but deliver us from the power of Satan and his host. For thine is the kingdom, power, strength, fortitude and dominion in heaven and on earth, now and always (he signs himself and raises his voice), world without end. (People or server) Amen."

Then, turning slightly to the west, the priest blesses the people: "Peace be with you," and they (server) respond: "And with thee and thy spirit."

The priest continues: "Holiness becometh the saints in the consummation, O Lord" (he kisses the altar), and the people (server) reply: "One holy Father, one holy Son, and one Holy Spirit. Glory be to the Father and to the Son and to the Holy Ghost, world without end. Amen."

The priest, bowing down over the altar and with his hands joined before his breast, now says: "Glory be to thee, God the Father; Glory be to thee, eternal Son; Glory be to thee, Holy Ghost by whom all is sanctified, world without end."

Then, moving the right hand [138] of the deacon to the altar, the priest says to him: "The grace of the Holy Ghost," and the minister replies: "Be with thee and with us, and with those that receive him in the kingdom of heaven, world without end. Amen."

The priest, having genuflected, says the *Domine non sum dignus*," as in the Roman rite, but the celebrant holds

[138] The *paroissien* of 1917 says: "Touching the hand of the server on the altar."

[139] In the rite of Braga, the priest holds the host at the *Domine non sum dignus*, in such a way that "those who are near may see it and adore."

in his left hand the broken host [139] in the form of a cross, striking his breast with the right.

The deacon (server) answers: "May this sacrifice be accepted on high, with the sacrifice of Abel, Noe and Abraham, in the heavenly home."

Then, placing the two halves of the host one over the other in his left hand, the priest says: "Let not, O Lord, let not, O Lord, thy body be to me unto condemnation, but unto the forgiveness of debts and the pardon of sins (repeated three times). Sanctify our bodies by thy sacred body, and pardon our debts by thy precious blood, and purify our consciences with the sprinkling of thy goodness, O Christ the hope of our nature, Lord of all, Father, Son and Holy Ghost."

The priest, signing himself with the host, receives it in communion, as he says: "May the body of our Lord Jesus Christ preserve my soul to life everlasting. Amen. Lord, I am not worthy that thou shouldst enter under my roof; say but the word and my soul shall live."

Then the deacon exclaims: "Bless, Lord," and the priest, having wiped his fingers and genuflected, turns to the people and blesses them: "May the gift of the grace † of our Lord Jesus Christ, the giver of life, be perfected by his mercy in all of us."

The people (server) respond: "For ever, world without end. Amen."

The priest, again genuflecting, receives the chalice and, having signed himself, says: "What shall I render to the Lord for all he hath rendered to me? I will take the chalice of salvation and call upon the name of the Lord. May the blood of our Lord Jesus Christ preserve my soul to life everlasting. Amen."

A rubric in the missal of 1912 directs that a lector,

doctor or deacon [140] shall now say: "My brethren, receive the body of the Son, says the Church, and drink his chalice with faith in the kingdom of heaven."

When holy communion is given, the deacon (server), as in the Roman rite, recites the *confiteor*, with the addition of the name of St. Thomas.

The *indulgentiam* is concluded with the words "Father, Son and Holy Ghost, world without end." "Behold the Lamb of God" and "Lord, I am not worthy" are also said.

Communion is given under one kind, with the following formula: "May the body of our Lord Jesus Christ be to the chaste priest ("cleric of God" or "pious faithful"), unto the forgiveness of sins and life everlasting. Amen."

The communicants then receive a blessing: "May the blessing of God the Father almighty, and of the Son, and of the Holy Ghost, descend upon you and remain in your hearts for ever. (Deacon or server) Amen."

A hymn is sung by the deacon or server: (On feasts) "Strengthen, [141] O Lord, the hands which are stretched out to receive the holy thing." (On Sundays) "Jesus, our Lord and our adorable King."

(On ferial days and at the commemoration of the dead): "May the mysteries we received with faith be to us, O Lord, unto the forgiveness of sins. Thou art the likeness alike of the servant and of the Creator, O Christ, King of ages. With thy body and blood thou didst purify the stains and forgive the debts of all who believed in thee. Make us all worthy to come to thee with confidence on the day of thy manifestation, and to offer thee praise with the hosts of angels. Amen, Amen."

---

[140] The *paroissien* of 1917 says " server."
[141] Sec Chaldean rite.

The priest, in the meanwhile, says secretly: "Let not thy living body, O Lord, which we have eaten, and the immaculate blood which we have drunk, turn to our judgment and condemnation, nor to our weakness and infirmity, but may it avail for the forgiveness of debts, the remission of sins, and confidence in thy sight, O Christ, the hope of our nature, Lord of all, Father, Son and Holy Ghost."

The ablutions are taken as in the Roman rite. At the purification of the chalice, the priest says:

> And we will greet thee with gladness.
> "In us who took thy body exteriorly
> May thy virtue dwell interiorly;
> And thrice sing praises to thee,
> With the just who fulfil thy will.

O Christ our nature's hope, Lord of all, Father, Son and Holy Ghost, world without end."

Then, at the purifying of the fingers: "Make us, who received thy body from the paten, and drank thy blood from the chalice, worthy to sing thy praises with the good thief in paradise, in company with the just who do thy will, O Christ, the hope of our nature, Lord of all, world without end. Amen."

The deacon (server), having removed the missal to the epistle side of the altar, recites: "Let us all, therefore, who by the gift of the grace of the Holy Ghost, approached and were made worthy to participate in these holy mysteries—glorious, life-giving and divine—thank and praise together God their giver."

The people answer: "Praise be to him for his unspeakable goodness," and the deacon (server) says: "Let us pray. Peace be with us."

Then the priest with extended hands continues: (Sundays and feasts) "Every day it is proper, at all times (re-

peated), it is meet, and at every hour it is just, that we confess, adore and glorify the awe-inspiring name of thy majesty.
For, through thy grace, O Lord, and through thy mercy,
thou didst make the weak nature of the sons of mortal men
worthy to bless thy name with the angels, and to be made
partakers in the mysteries of thy gift, to be delighted with
the sweetness of thy life-giving and divine words, and to
sing for ever the hymn of praise and glory to thy Godhead,
Lord of all, Father, Son and Holy Ghost."

The deacon (server) responds: "Amen. Be pleased,
Lord, to give thy blessing," and the priest says: "May Christ
our God and our Lord, our King and our Saviour, and the
giver of our life, who by his goodness made us worthy to
receive his body and precious blood, which sanctifies all
things, grant us the grace to please him in word and deed,
in thought and action. May this pledge which we have received and are receiving avail to us, O Lord, for the forgiveness of debts and the remission of sins, for the great
hope of resurrection from the dead, and for the new life in
the kingdom of heaven, with all those who pleased thee
through thy grace and goodness, world without end. Amen."

On ferial days, a shorter form is used: (Priest) "We
ought to offer, O Lord, to thy most blessed Trinity, glory
and honour, praise, adoration and perpetual thanksgiving
for the gift of the holy mysteries—glorious, life-giving and
divine—which thou in thy goodness didst give us for the
forgiveness of our sins, by thy grace and mercy, Lord of
all, Father, Son and Holy Ghost."

(Deacon or server) "Amen. Be pleased, Lord, to give
thy blessing." (Priest) "Blessed be thy adorable gift, O
Christ, from thy place on high, which gives pardon to our
debts and our sins, and blots out our offences by the virtue
of the holy mysteries—glorious, life-giving and divine—,O

Christ the hope of our nature, world without end. Amen."

The priest and deacon (server) now join together in the Lord's prayer, and the priest "prays for the deacon" ("server"): "May our Lord Jesus Christ, to whom we ministered, whom we served and honoured, by his holy mysteries—glorious, life-giving and divine—make us worthy of the magnificent glory of his kingdom, of happiness with his holy angels, and of confidence in his presence, and that we may stand at his right hand in the heavenly Jerusalem. May his mercy and goodness be poured out upon us and upon the whole world, upon the Church and her children, †
now and always, world without end."

The deacon (server) responds: "Be pleased, Lord, to give thy blessing."

A final hymn is recited by the priest, and the missal provides a number of alternatives.

That given here is taken from the *Paroissien* of 1917: "1) To him, who pardoned our debts by his body, and blotted out our sins by his blood, 2) be praises sung in his Church, and upon you, his blessed people and the sheep of his flock, 3) may he pour out his graces, and may he multiply in you his mercy and grace, 4) and may the right hand of his providence protect you now and always, world without end. (People or server) Amen."

Then, as in the Maronite and Syrian rites, the priest, kissing the altar, bids a farewell to the holy table: "Remain thou in peace, O altar of propitiation; remain thou in peace, O sepulchre of our Lord. May the oblation I received from thee avail for the forgiveness of my debts and the remission of my sins. I know not whether or no I shall come again and offer another sacrifice upon thee."

The missal of 1912 gives the following as an alternative concluding prayer: "As thou hast made us worthy, O Lord, to rejoice in thy body and holy blood, so also make us worthy to rejoice in that kingdom of thine which passeth not away and is not dissolved, with all thy saints, now and always .... ."

The Leonine prayers are recited at "low Mass."

BIBLIOGRAPHY.

1. *A Brief Sketch of the History of the St. Thomas Christians.* Fr. BERNARDUS OF ST. THOMAS. Trinchinopoly: St. Joseph's Industrial School Press. 1924.

2. *Christianity in Malabar* with special reference to the St. Thomas Christians of the Syro-Malabar Rite. Joseph C. PANJIKARAN. *Orientalia Christiana*, vol. VI, No. 23 (April 1926). Pontificale Institutum Orientalium Studiorum. Roma.

3. *The Christians of St. Thomas and their Liturgies.* George Broadley HOWARD. Oxford & London: John Henry & James Parker, 1864.

4. *The Church of SS. Thomas and Bartholomew in Malabar.* H. C. E. ZACHARIAS. *Pax.* The Quarterly Review of the Benedictines of Priknash. Spring (86) and Summer (87). 1928.

5. *Fontes Juris Canonici Syro-Malankarensium.* PLACIDUS A S. JOSEPH. Fonti. Serie II, fascicolo IX. Typis Polyglottis Vaticanis. 1940.

6. *De Fontibus Juris Ecclesiastici Syro-Malankarensium.* Commentarius Historico-Canonicus. PLACIDUS A S. JOSEPH. Fonti. Serie II, fascicolo VIII. Typis Polyglottis Vaticanis. 1937.

7. *Genuinae Relationes inter Sedem Apostolicam et Chaldaeorum Ecclesiam.* Cura et studio Samuel GIAMIL. Roma: Ermanno Loescher. 1902.

8. *Historia Ecclesiae Malabaricae cum Diamperitana synodo.* RAULIN. Rome. 1745.

9. *Jornada do arcebispo de Goa dom Frey Aleixo de Menezes.* Antonio DE GOUVEA. Coimbra. 1606.

10. *Malabar.* H. LECLERCQ. *Dictionnaire d'Archéologie Chrétienne et de Liturgie.* T. X, part. I, col. 1260-1277.

11. *Malabar Christians and their Ancient Documents.* T. K. JOSEPH OF TRAVANCORE. Trivandrum. 1929.

12. *Ordo Missae Syro-Chaldeo-Malabaricae* cum translatione Latina. Printed at M. T. S. Press. Puttenpally. 1912.

13. *The Syriac Mass.* Translated by John PALOCAREN. Trinchinopoly: St. Joseph's Industrial School Press. 1917.

14. *The Syrian Christians in Malabar.* Fr. BARTHOLOMEW OF JESUS. J. M. Suares. Codialbail Press. Mangalore.

ACKNOWLEDGEMENTS

1. Dr. Alexander Chulaparambil, Bishop of Kottayam.

CPSIA information can be obtained at www.ICGtesting.com
Printed in the USA
LVOW071602050812

293000LV00002B/234/P